The slave was not only physically ubiquitous but also a constant imaginative presence in the classical world. This book explores the presence of slaves and slavery in Roman literature and asks particularly what the free imagination made of the experience of living with slaves, beings who both were and were not fellow humans. As a shadow humanity, slaves furnished the free with other selves and imaginative alibis as well as mediators between and substitutes for their peers. As presences that witnessed their owners' most unguarded moments they possessed the knowledge that was the object of both curiosity and anxiety. William Fitzgerald discusses not only the ideological relations of Roman literature to the institution of slavery, but also the ways in which slavery provided a metaphor for a range of other relationships and experiences, and in particular for literature itself. The book is arranged thematically and covers a broad chronological and generic field.

WILLIAM FITZGERALD is Professor of Classics and Comparative Literature, University of California at San Diego. He is the author of *Agonistic Poetry: the Pindaric Mode in Pindar, Horace, Hoelderlin and the English Ode* (1987) and *Catullan Provocations: Lyric Poetry and the Drama of Position* (1995).

T0382534

ROMAN LITERATURE
AND ITS CONTEXTS

Slavery and the Roman Literary Imagination

ROMAN LITERATURE
AND ITS CONTEXTS

Series editors
Denis Feeney and Stephen Hinds

This series promotes approaches to Roman literature which are open to dialogue with current work in other areas of the classics, and in the humanities at large. The pursuit of contacts with cognate fields such as social history, anthropology, history of thought, linguistics and literary theory is in the best traditions of classical scholarship: the study of Roman literature, no less than Greek, has much to gain from engaging with these other contexts and intellectual traditions. The series offers a forum in which readers of Latin texts can sharpen their readings by placing them in broader and better-defined contexts, and in which other classicists and humanists can explore the general or particular implications of their work for readers of Latin texts. The books all constitute original and innovative research and are envisaged as suggestive essays whose aim is to stimulate debate.

Other books in the series

Slavery and the Roman Literary Imagination

WILLIAM FITZGERALD

University of California at San Diego

CAMBRIDGE UNIVERSITY PRESS
Cambridge, New York, Melbourne, Madrid, Cape Town, Singapore,
São Paulo, Delhi, Dubai, Tokyo, Mexico City

Cambridge University Press
The Edinburgh Building, Cambridge CB2 8RU, UK

Published in the United States of America by
Cambridge University Press, New York

www.cambridge.org
Information on this title: www.cambridge.org/9780521779692

First published 2000

A catalogue record for this publication is available from the British Library

Library of Congress Cataloguing in Publication data

Fitzgerald, William, 1952–
    Slavery and the Roman literary imagination / William Fitzgerald.
    p.   cm. – (Roman literature and its contexts)
    Includes bibliographical references and index.
    ISBN 0 521 77031 9 (hardback) – ISBN 0 521 77969 2 (paperback)
    1. Latin literature – History and criticism.   2. Slavery in literature.
 3. Slavery – Rome – History.   4. Slaves – Rome.   I. Title.   II. Series.

PA6030.S6 F58 2000
870.9´3520625 21–dc21   99-016685

ISBN 978-0-521-77031-6 Hardback
ISBN 978-0-521-77969-2 Paperback

For Kathy

Contents

Acknowledgments

I am deeply grateful to the editors of this series, Denis Feeney and Stephen Hinds, for conceiving of the format that inspired this book, for their encouragement and support, and for the generous care they gave to reading an earlier draft. Many suggestions they made have been incorporated into the final version. Kathleen McCarthy was kind enough to show me work in progress from her forthcoming book on Plautus; she also read a previous draft and made some valuable comments. The influence of her insight and acuity will be readily apparent throughout this manuscript. P. G. McC. Brown read the manuscript in an earlier incarnation and saved me from a number of errors; the fact that I have persisted in my recklessness in some places is my fault and not his. The two anonymous readers for the Press helped to make this a better book than it would otherwise have been with their criticisms, suggestions and bibliographical expertise. I am grateful to both of them. Pauline Hire and Muriel Hall were both exemplary editors. Finally, the dedicatee gave me the benefit of her editorial skills, and it is to her that I owe the happy circumstances in which this book was written.

Introduction: living with slaves

For the citizens of ancient Athens and Rome, a life without slaves would have been unthinkable, literally so.[1] Not only did slaves perform a vast range of work for the majority of the population, but classical thought was permeated by the category of the slave. Ancient Greek and Roman writers made a stark opposition between free and slave, without nuances;[2] when looking at other cultures, they could see only slaves and free – other statuses they ignored or assimilated to slavery.[3] Freedom was a crucial political slogan of both societies, and the freedom of the citizen was sharpened by and contrasted with the servility of the slave, an outsider: in the Twelve Tables it was stipulated that Romans who had been enslaved had to be sold "across the Tiber," and after Solon's abolition of debt-bondage no Athenian citizen could be enslaved within the community.[4] Within the community of the free, distinctions were made between "liberal" and "illiberal" behavior, demeanor and, most notoriously, means of earning a living, so that physical work performed for others was stigmatized by its association with slaves.[5] The influence of slavery on ancient culture can be traced in everything from Plato's cosmology and the Roman concept of legal ownership (*dominium*) to the Cupids of Campanian painting.[6]

---

[1] Garlan (1988),126–38 on imaginary slaveless societies, excluded from the natural order and historical time.   [2] Finley (1981),116.

[3] Wiedemann (1987), 5; de Ste Croix (1981),173.

[4] Wirszubski (1960) on Rome, and Raaflaub (1985) on Greece.

[5] Finley (1973), 72–6; Joshel (1992), 66–8 on the *locus classicus*, Cicero's *De Officiis* 150–1.

[6] See Vlastos (1941) on Plato; Patterson (1982) on *dominium*, 30; Slater (1974) for an argument that the Cupids are inspired by the fashion of keeping slave children around the house to amuse the master or mistress.

This book is about the presence of slavery in Roman literature and the title of this introduction, "Living with Slaves," indicates two things about the scope of the subject: first of all, it is restricted to the perspective of the slave-owners and, secondly, it focuses on the domestic sphere. These are the main biases of the surviving material, worth dwelling on for a moment.

Nothing that could be called a slave literature survives from antiquity.[7] The rich tradition of American slave narratives and oral histories of ex-slaves, the preserved music and songs of slaves, all these allow us to reconstruct some picture of the slaves' experience and culture in the antebellum South. Very little can be done in this respect for the Roman slave.[8] This is not because slaves and ex-slaves didn't write – Roman literature and intellectual life would be considerably poorer were it not for the slaves who participated in it.[9] Many important figures in Roman cultural life were slaves or freedmen: Livius Andronicus, Terence, Publilius Syrus, Phaedrus, and Epictetus, for instance. Some of these figures, and many others who did not achieve such prominence, had been educated at their masters' expense in order to perform secretarial, educational or cultural work, another difference from the American South, where anti-literacy laws existed, even if they were often flouted.[10] But slavery was too much an unquestioned part of the way things were for the experience of the slave to be conceived as an object of interest. There were no abolitionist audiences eager to hear what this pernicious institution does to the people involved in it; there was no turning-point that made the world of slavery a thing of the past, leaving a bitter legacy with which the present had to come to terms.[11] Furthermore, slaves came from almost every part of the world with which the Romans came into contact, another difference from slavery in the antebellum South, and a fact that militated against the development of a slave culture. Since Roman slavery was not racial in essence, ex-slaves were considerably better integrated into (slave-owning) society than the African-American slave: formally manumitted slaves became Roman citizens,[12] and they

---

[7] With the possible exception of the animal fable. See chapter 5.

[8] But see Bömer (1981), Joshel (1992), Kudlien (1991), and Bradley (1994).

[9] For a negative view, see Pliny *N.H.* 35.58. In the time of Hadrian, Hermippus of Berytus, himself a freedman, wrote a book *About Slaves Eminent in Learning.*

[10] Booth (1979), schooling of slaves; Wiedemann (1987), 38, *vernae* taught Greek literature; Genovese (1972), 561–6 on anti-literacy laws in the South.

[11] On ancient critiques of slavery, see Cambiano (1987) and Garnsey (1996), 75–86.

[12] Fabre (1981), 5–39 and Gardner (1993), 8–11.

spoke with the voice of the masters.[13] If we are looking for the slave's story in literature, we have to content ourselves with scraps like Trimalchio's thumbnail autobiography in Petronius' *Satyricon*, or, as I will argue in chapter 5, a fantastic tale like Apuleius' *Golden Ass*, both written by free men. This study, then, is concerned with the writing and the perspective of the masters; needless to say, that does not mean it must reproduce them.

The second bias of the material is its concern with a particular sub-section of the slave population, the domestic slaves. It is impossible to quantify the total slave population in Italy accurately, but recent esti-mates stand at two or three million by the end of the first century BCE (between thirty and forty per cent of the population).[14] Ownership of slaves, or a slave, was spread across the population: at the top of the scale, households of several hundred slaves are reported, but even the poor peasant in the pseudo-Virgilian *Moretum*, who lives alone, is given a (black) slave by the poem's author. Below him socially, even slaves could "own" slaves (*vicarii*).[15] Slaves were employed in all kinds of work, often side by side with the free, from the most menial to the most intellectual,[16] but the most important categorical distinction in Roman thought was between the rural and the urban slaves. Literature has far less to say about the rural slaves than the urban, and the former remain an anonymous, faceless mass in the Roman writers. Virgil's great poem on agriculture, for instance, makes no mention of the slave laborers that would have worked the estates he is describing, though they may be implied by the military metaphors that pepper the text of the *Georgics*.[17] The agricultural writers Varro, Cato and Columella tell us quite a lot about the management of slaves on farms, and they make it clear that the life of a slave on the farm was harsh. One of the most dreaded punishments for the domestic slave in literature was banishment to the country estate or, worse, to the mill. Without the close interaction with the master that the domestic slave might enjoy there was less chance of manumission, or adoption, which

---

[13] Treggiari (1969), 241–3. But see also Christes (1979), Bloomer (1997), 73–109 (on Phaedrus) and Bradley (1994), 174–8.

[14] Brunt (1971), 121–30 and Hopkins (1978), 9. Scheidel (1997) estimates 6 million out of a total population of 60 million in the Roman empire of the Principate.

[15] On the pattern of slave holding, Bradley (1994), 10–12; on *vicarii*, Buckland (1908), 239–49.   [16] Bradley (1994), 58–65.

[17] And by the bees in Book 4; see Fitzgerald (1996), 394 (and compare Horace *Epode* 2. 65–6, *vernas, ditis examen domus*).

was what launched Trimalchio on his career.[18] On the other hand, there was also less exposure to the whims and moods of cruel masters and mistresses.[19] Not surprisingly, it was the interaction between domestic slave and master that most interested the Roman writers.

In spite of this interest we know much too little about the physical details of the cohabitation of slaves and free in the Roman house. To what extent there were separate slave quarters or rooms is not clear, though Roman notions of privacy were very different from our own: literary evidence suggests that at least some slaves slept in the same rooms as their masters or mistresses, or just outside the door.[20] Artemidorus, the second-century dream interpreter, identifies mice appearing in dreams as domestic slaves, since slaves live with us, share the same food, and are cowardly (3.28). It is auspicious to dream of lots of mice, happy and playing, since this augurs a good atmosphere among the slaves and an increase in their numbers. Seneca, urging familiar relations with slaves in the famous *Letter* 47, insists against an imaginary interlocutor ("But they're slaves") that slaves are *contubernales*, "housemates," a word whose first meaning is "sharers of a tent" (comrades in arms) and which also means the "mate" of a slave. Serving as a soldier and marrying are two statuses restricted to the free, so Seneca's usage reminds us of the distinction between slave and free at the same time as it tries to bridge the gap. He praises Lucilius because he lives *familiariter* ("intimately") with his slaves, again making a daring suggestion by means of a term that has a special meaning in relation to slaves – it is both extraordinary and self-evident that Lucilius would live *familiariter* with his *familia* (slaves).

The Roman concepts of the *domus* and the *familia*, both of which may include relations *and* slaves, indicate that on some level slaves and free living under the same roof formed a unit.[21] Seneca cites *familiaritas* as a reason to be lenient with a slave (*De Ira* 3.24.20) and evidence that the *familia*, free and slaves, formed an affective unit is not hard to come by: one might cite, for instance, the importance attached to the distinction

[18] Varro (1.17.5) and Columella (1.8) assume that even the *vilici* (overseers) will be slaves; see Wiedemann (1985),163.

[19] Aristotle, *Politics* 1263a, "we collide most with those of our servants whom we employ most often for everyday attendance."

[20] George (1997) and Wallace-Hadrill (1994), 38–44.

[21] Saller (1994), chapter 4, and (1987), 67.

between the houseborn slave (*verna*) and the bought slave.[22] Cato the Elder had his wife suckle and raise the slave children with her son "so as to encourage brotherly feelings in them towards her own son."[23]

The range of meanings that a life with slaves had for the free was extremely broad and it is appropriate that the English phrase "living with slaves" can be understood in several ways, all relevant to Roman slavery. For instance, masters lived with slaves as one eats with a fork, maintaining a civilized style of life; or they lived with slaves as one "lives with" death, since slaves provided a constant reminder of something terrible that might befall any of them; or they learnt to live with slaves as one learns to live with children, putting up with their childish ways with amused resignation. In some ways, slaves constituted a shadow humanity, both substitutes for and extensions of the free: a slave-owner might have relationships with slaves as paramours, concubines or foster-children (*delicati, concubinae, alumni*) that echoed, however faintly, their relations with other free people; as agents (*actores*), messengers, attendants (*pedisequae*) and the like slaves acted as proxies for their masters. Furthermore, like shadows, slaves were a supplement necessary to the self-image and identity of their masters and mistresses.

Patterson's illuminating comparative study (1982) shows that the function of slavery is by no means exclusively utilitarian; as beings deprived of honor, slaves serve to bolster the honor of their masters. In ancient Rome, they allowed the rich to live nobly, and to do so without degrading the free poor.[24] When Petronius' Eumolpus pretends to be a shipwrecked millionaire, he claims that it is not the loss of property that concerns him, but the fact that without slaves he cannot recognize his own dignity (*sed destitutum ministerio non agnoscere dignitatem suam*, 117). Significantly, many of the names that were popularly given to slaves were taken from the world of Greek mythology; to call a slave Achilles, Pallas, Ajax, Dionysus or Paris was not simply to make a sarcastic joke, for slaves allowed their masters to share in the civilized world of which Greek culture was the most precious fruit (compare the Pompeys and Catos of the antebellum

---

[22] Tacitus *Annals* 14.44, Statius *Silvae* 2.1.72–8. On *empticius servus*, see Kudlien (1986).

[23] Plutarch *Cato Maior* 20.3, cf. 4.4; 21. On evidence from magic, see Kudlien (1991).

[24] Hopkins (1978), 112. Athenaeus 272 e and 273 b-c, on ostentation as the purpose of slaves.

South).[25] In the decorum of epic poetry, the flame that cooks the hero's food is Hephaestus, the water in which he bathes a nymph, and so on; surrounded by minions, often bearing the names of deities and heroes from Greek literature, who mediated between him and the material world, the Roman slave-owner breathed the air of culture, shielded from sordid reality.[26] Trimalchio, Petronius' vulgarian freedman, takes this all too literally: his *sommelier* is Liber, the name of the Roman Dionysus, whom he punningly liberates, and his carver is Ajax, who enters just as Trimalchio is discoursing, with sovereign ignorance, about the original – "But he'll show you himself" (59). Seneca (*Ep.* 27) tells us that a certain Sabinus, "who inherited a freedman's wealth and his mind too" (5), had slaves memorize the Greek literature of which he was ignorant and supply him with apt quotations at dinner.

Living with contradiction

At the most basic level, slaves were there to do things that the free couldn't, or wouldn't, do for themselves. School exercises surviving from late antiquity, but probably containing material from earlier periods, show that an important component of learning language was learning to order slaves around.[27] Every activity would be accompanied by a flurry of imperatives. Among other things, slaves were instruments for living, and Varro's notorious definition of the slave as a "speaking instrument" (*instrumentum vocale, R.R.* 1.17.1) encapsulates a ruthlessness that was not restricted to the manuals on farming, in which the slave is viewed simply as an economic factor. That humans could be cast in this role is one of the worst consequences of slavery, but Varro's much-quoted phrase cannot be taken to tell the whole story about how the slave was regarded by the slave-owning class. Varro's definition is often cited alongside a passage from Aristotle's *Politics* (1253b) in which the slave is defined as "an animate piece of property," and a piece of property as "a tool to live with." As with the Varro quotation, it would be a gross misrepresentation to take this definition out of its technical context and say that slaves were not thought of, or treated, as human. It may well be that the institution of slavery makes possible treatises on crafts in which

---

[25] On slave nomenclature, see Gordon (1968).
[26] Fitzgerald (1996), 405–6 (on *Moretum*). [27] Dionisotti (1982), 93.

people are defined in terms of their functions, but neither Varro nor Aristotle are defining the slave *tout court*. When a character in Juvenal asks "Since when is a slave human?" (6.222), she has already been marked as a monster. Though the slave's humanity was philosophically and legally problematic – and this licensed a great deal of appalling treatment – slave-owners knew that their slaves were humans as well as chattel, and in this respect living with slaves involved living with contradiction. Some aspects of the practice and law of slavery assumed the instrumental status of the slave as chattel, but others emphasized the slave's humanity: the institution was contradictory, and no simple characterization or definition could possibly be adequate to Roman attitudes to slaves.[28] This book, then, does not aim to formulate those attitudes, but rather to locate the paradoxes and ambiguities that made this complex institution such a rich literary subject.

A good example of the ambiguous status of the slave's humanity is the problem of whether a slave could exercise virtue. Aristotle raises this when he distinguishes the slave from the artisan and mechanic in respect of the virtue that rubs off on the slave as "sharer of the life" (κοινωνὸς ζωῆς) of his master.[29] The slave both does and doesn't share the moral world of the master. Dupont (1992) characterizes the negative case well: "In Roman eyes a slave that cleaves to his master throughout the latter's life, who only acts on command and who is a mere extension to the citizen's body, although certainly a man, is a man bereft of moral independence; he is cut off from his past and his will is broken. We can see that a slave, therefore, is a man with no *animus*" (57). But if the slave is in a position to display loyalty to his master in times of danger (i.e. to do more than act on command), then he or she must be accorded the capacity to exercise virtue. Roman jurists, perhaps sensing this problem, made it obligatory for a slave to come to the aid of a master in danger.[30] But when Seneca tackles the issue of whether a slave has the capacity to confer a *beneficium* on his master, he comes down firmly in favor, and is able to draw on a wealth of anecdotes about slaves faithful beyond the call of duty (*De Beneficiis* 3.18– 27).[31] What I want to emphasize here is

[28] Dumont (1987), 96–106 on law and the humanity of the slave.
[29] *Politics* 1260a, discussed by de Ste Croix (1981), 184–5.
[30] Norden (1912), 67–8.
[31] On anecdotes about faithful slaves, see Parker (1998).

that the cohabitation of slave and master generated a set of problems about the moral status of the slave that could not be definitively solved, and that it is more fruitful to see the master's (and probably the slave's) experience of slavery in terms of such conflicts than in terms of fixed attitudes, especially when one is dealing with literature.

The individual chapters of this book focus on particular aspects of the master's or mistress's experience, real or imaginary, of living with slaves. Each chapter reads the imaginative structure of some aspect of this experience through literary texts. In the first chapter, I look at the slave as an other self, and in the third as a substitute for, or mediator between, free people; chapter 2 focuses on the slave as the person who is both punished and, at the same time, licensed to misbehave; chapter 4 considers slavery as a yardstick and metaphor for other relationships, and chapter 5 examines enslavement and, briefly, manumission, as a locus of concern about social mobility expressed through images of metamorphosis and hybridity.

Slavery and literature

Though it may supply us with much important information about slavery, literature cannot provide us with a picture of "how it actually was." Quite apart from the fact that it only gives us half the story – the slave's experience goes unrepresented – literature was itself one of the ways that Roman masters lived with slavery, and literary stylization a means of negotiating the meanings that slavery generated.[32] Literature about slavery, then, is ideological in the broad sense in which ideology is "the indispensable medium in which individuals live out their relationship to a social structure."[33] Reading the literature of slavery will involve, for a start, some consideration of ideology in the narrower senses in which literature serves to confirm the official line on the nature and status of slaves and to naturalize the institution and its practices. There was, for instance, a pervasive set of oppositions inherited from Athenian thought that legitimated the master's domination of the slave as part of the order of things: thus, slavery is to freedom as incontinence is to self-control and emotions are to bodily appetite; the slave is to the master as body is to

---

[32] Hopkins (1993), 1, n. 33.
[33] Eagleton (1991), 1–2 distinguishes sixteen senses of "ideology" of which this is one.

mind, as woman is to man, and child to father.[34] These oppositions, as we shall see, are omnipresent in the literature of slavery. Wiles' (1988) study of the legitimation of slavery in Menander plots some of these oppositions onto the distribution and typology of comic masks, showing how they situate the slave in his or her place in the natural order of things. It is against the stable background of this structure of types that the slave can act contrary to type without upsetting the order nature intends but that, as Aristotle regretted (*Politics* 1254b), is not always realized.

But there are many official lines, serving various purposes, and not infrequently they conflict with one another. The institution of slavery, which even Roman jurists recognized as "contrary to nature," (Florentinus, *Dig.*1.5.4.1) was riven with contradictions, ambiguities and ironies. That people can hold contradictory beliefs is well attested and will surprise no one, but literature is preeminently the place where such complexities are expressed, exploited and managed. A recent article by W. Thalmann (1997) on Plautus' *Captivi* provides an exemplary study of this aspect of literature's ideological function, showing how the play negotiates the contradictions between two widely held views of slavery, which Thalmann calls the "suspicious" and the "benevolent" models respectively. According to the former, the slave is inherently untrustworthy, and master-slave relations are necessarily based on force and mistrust; according to the latter, the slave is potentially content with his lot and faithful, so that master-slave relations are assimilated to kinship.[35] The one justifies enslavement (of inherently base people) and the other has persuasive, and self-congratulatory, force. In *Captivi* the vicissitudes of war enslave master and slave together, and they engage in a scheme to return home that involves exchanging roles, which means that they must trust each other; the slave (Tyndarus) remains faithful to his master, while the master is true to his paternal role. Tyndarus, as the audience knows all along, is in fact of free birth, so it is never quite clear whether he is acting as a faithful slave or a morally superior free person. But by playing the faithful Tyndarus off against Stalagmus, the bad slave who kidnapped Tyndarus in the first place, Plautus allows both suspicious and benevolent models of slavery to hold. As Thalmann puts it (130): "in the *Captivi* hierarchical structures, as crystallized in the master-slave relation, are

---

[34] Just (1985); Murnaghan and Joshel (1998).
[35] Compare Wiedemann (1985),163–7 on the benevolent model.

temporarily relaxed, or at least seen as not inevitable, through the displacement of persons and the evident interchangeability of roles, and then redrawn all the more firmly in the play's ending."[36]

This kind of ideological analysis might also be applied to particular literary slave types. Sandra Joshel has shown that the nurse comes in good and bad versions, like Thalmann's suspicious and benevolent models of slavery.[37] The figure of the loyal and loving "good" nurse, almost a mother, serves to occlude the resentment of outsiders forced to serve in the *domus*. The "bad" nurse (the nurse as advisor in tragedy and elegy), perverting the role of mother who properly accommodates her daughter to male control (10), expresses some of the anxiety at foreign elements infiltrating a culture whose imperial growth had profoundly disturbed its sense of identity. Here again, literature allows the cake to be both had and eaten.

Though all literature involves ideology in some sense, this doesn't mean that literary works must be read toward the kind of ideological closure that Thalmann finds in *Captivi*. Even if the ending of the play neatly ties things up, it does not follow that the work as a whole is closed, or that the questioning of natural hierarchies implied by all the social role-playing it stages has been neutralized. Literary works are overdetermined and their figurative play seldom holds stable, which is why any particular work is likely to furnish the means to deconstruct its own ideological implications. Reading the literature of slavery, then, will also involve reading its exposure of the gaps and rifts in ideology, its capacity to let the unspeakable be spoken, to assert what it apparently denies, and this too will be part of my project.

Slavery is not the only subject of the literature of slavery. As humans shadowing, extending and coming between the free, slaves allowed the free to imagine being otherwise, furnishing them with an imaginative alibi. Let us take, for instance, the comedies of Plautus, which confront us with extraordinarily self-confident and impertinent slaves. According to Donatus (*Ad Eunuchum*, 57), it was permissible to present slaves cleverer than their masters in comedies played in Greek dress (*palliatae*), but

---

[36] McCarthy (forthcoming) finds a different, but analogous, conflict negotiated in the same play, namely that between the slave as transferable goods and as faithful servant, a conflict played out in Tyndarus' deception of his new master for the benefit of his old one.   [37] Joshel (1986), 6–11.

not in comedies in Roman dress (*togatae*); in fact, there are signs in the extant remains that the clever slave featured in *togatae* too, but Donatus' statement provides an interesting glimpse of anxiety about these figures.[38] Doubtless slaves at Rome did resist and manipulate their masters to the best of their ability,[39] but Plautus' clever slaves are not just portraits, however exaggerated, of that resistance. These lovable tricksters in their imaginary Greek setting can be read, among other things, as fantasy projections of the free, not so much portraits of slaves as others through whom the free could play out their own agenda. Slavery, as a polar opposite of the free state, could be the place where the free imagined escaping from the demands of "liberal" comportment and indulging in revolt against their own superiors.[40] Furthermore, as an extreme condition, slavery confronted the free with the constant presence of humanity at its limits, a humanity against which they could measure themselves.[41] "Even slaves have always had the liberty to feel hope or fear or joy or sorrow of their own impulse, not someone else's" writes C. Matius to Cicero, (*Ad Fam.*11.28.3) and Seneca argues that a slave can confer a *beneficium* in order to claim this privilege, *a fortiori*, for sons (*De Beneficiis* 3.29.1).

Finally, an account of slavery and literature must consider the availability of slavery as a model or metaphor for other institutions. Slavery did, or could, make everything else look different. Some of what literature has to tell us about slavery, then, concerns the fact that slaves were good to think with, and one of the things about which slaves helped the Romans to think was literature itself. Stephen Hinds has recently argued that Martial's slaves masturbating at the keyhole while Hector and Andromache make love (11.104.13–14) are figures of the poet's licentious Muse (and the prurient reader?).[42] We will see that the metatheatrical antics of the plotting Plautine slave, the artistry of the maid of Ovid's mistress, and the eavesdropping of the metamorphosed Lucius, who narrates his adventures as beast of burden in Apuleius' *Golden Ass*, all serve to reflect something of the literary itself through the peculiar position and ambiguous status of the slave.

---

[38] The fragments of *togata* are collected in Daviault (1981); on slaves, see Daviault 23 n.3 and 44 n.12 (on Donatus), and in the fragments, see especially Afranius 193–5 and 256.   [39] Bradley (1994), 107–31.

[40] A central point of McCarthy (forthcoming), discussed in chapter 2 below.

[41] Wiedemann (1987), 13.   [42] Hinds (1998), 134–5.

Each of these approaches to the reading of literature about slaves will be found in this book, but there are other legitimate questions and topics that will not be pursued. The individual chapters range widely over several centuries, and to many it will be a fault that I have little to say about the changing historical context. Another book would (and I hope will) look at the diachronic aspects of the tradition. Certainly, the late Republic and early Empire changed the implications of slavery for the elite Roman, as I will indicate, but a more precise articulation of the literature of slavery with the changing situations of the elite and the changing nature of slavery will have to await another study. I suspect, though, that there is more continuity than change both in the circumstances of slavery and in the literature about it.[43] The particular arrangement and juxtaposition of works that I have adopted is intended to take them out of their more familiar historical, generic or authorial contexts and to suggest categories through which we can read their contribution to a different agenda.

[43] As Robbins points out in his book on the servant in the modern novel, continuity is also an historical phenomenon. Robbins (1986) 33, citing Said, and 131–2, citing Jameson.

The other self: proximity
and symbiosis

Aristotle (*Politics* 1255b) says of the slave that he is "part of the master – he is, as it were, a part of the body, alive yet separated from it." The symbiosis of master and slave is the subject of this chapter, a paradoxical symbiosis between the master and his "separate part" that expresses itself in complementarities, reversals and appropriations. This symbiosis, and the attendant ironies of domination, are central to the European tradition of literature about servants, passing from the ancient literature into Cervantes' Sancho Panza and Don Quixote, Diderot's Jacques and his master, Wodehouse's Jeeves and Wooster and a host of other pairs; it is epitomized by Hegel's discussion of the dialectic of slave and master in the *Phenomenology*.[1]

Aristotle might have added that the slave is part of the master's *mind* as well as his body, both an unruly part of the master's knowledge of himself and, by virtue of the huge difference in status, a parodic version of the master's knowledge of the world. For the slaves in this chapter (with one exception) it is manifestly *not* true that "a slave does not know his master's business" (John 15.15). Some slaves, of course, were deeply involved in their masters' business, performing crucial tasks as secretary and amanuensis.[2] Cicero's Tiro is a famous example. Just how indispensable such a slave could become is graphically shown by the letters (collected in *ad Fam.* 16) that Cicero wrote to Tiro, whom he freed in 53, and the master's love for his (now ex-) slave is vividly expressed in the letters he wrote when Tiro was dangerously ill with malaria. Pliny (*Ep.*7.4) quotes an erotic poem written by the great man to his slave, a poem suggesting at the least

---

[1] Hegel (1977), 111–19.   [2] On secretaries, Teitler (1985).

that an atmosphere of free badinage prevailed between them. Tiro's legacy to the future was the invention of the first system of tachygraphy (*Tironianae notae*), and one of the most poignant representations of the need that the master might develop for a trusted slave is the epitaph for one of Tiro's descendants, the slave-stenographer Xanthias, whose life was cut off prematurely. Xanthias' epitaph (*CIL* 13.8355) was found in Cologne, preceded by the unfinished epitaph of another slave:[3]

> hoc carmen, haec ara, hic cinis
> pueri sepulcrum est Xantiae,
> qui morte acerba raptus est,
> iam doctus in compendia
> tot literarum et nominum
> notare currenti stilo
> quod lingua currens diceret.
> iam nemo superaret legens,
> iam voce erili coeperat
> ad omne dictatum volans
> aurem vocari at proximam.
> heu morte propera concidit
> arcana qui solus sui
> sciturus domini fuit.

> This poem, this altar, this ash
> is the tomb of Xanthias,
> who was taken away by bitter death,
> already skilled at abbreviating
> so many letters and words,
> he could transcribe with fluent pen
> what the fluent tongue had said.
> Already he was second to none at reading,
> already he had begun to be summoned
> to be his master's closest ear,
> flying to every dictate of his master's voice.
> Alas, he succumbed to hasty death,
> he who alone would have known
> his master's intimate thoughts.

[3] Text, translation and commentary in Courtney 1995 (no.131).

Compassion for Xanthias, cut off before he attained the position in his master's confidence that might have earned him his freedom, is mingled with regret on the part of the master – regret that the person who alone would have known his secrets has died before being called to the position of confidant. The voice of this kind of funerary inscription hovers somewhere between that of Xanthias speaking of himself in the third person to a passer-by, of the master speaking of his own loss, and of some impersonal speaker reflecting on a poignant fate. The final *heu* is spoken from all three perspectives. For the impersonal speaker, there are ironies in the situation: the boy's powers of abbreviation are trumped by death who, like the boy, is also in a hurry (*propera*, 12; cf. *currenti*, 6 and *volans*, 10); as the boy rushes to keep up with his master, death outruns him. But perhaps hurrying has been the death of him, and he died by "a hurrying death" (*propera morte*). It is as though the preternatural speed with which the boy keeps up with his master's voice is demanded by the social distance between them, the ground that must be made up before intimacy can arise. The very effort that is required to bridge this gap in nature is dangerous. Did the boy know how close he was to his master's confidence? Perhaps not, but the emergence of mutuality out of the servile relationship is beautifully caught in lines 9–11: rushing to every word of his master's voice, the slave finds this very voice calling him to the master's closest *ear* (whether to be his master's ear, or to have his master's ear is not entirely clear).

It was supposedly characteristic of the free man to walk at a moderate pace, displaying the appropriate *constantia*, and characteristic of the slave going about his errands to run.[4] In fact, the entry of the running slave, clearing a path for himself, became one of the most hackneyed jokes of ancient comedy.[5] Here the running slave (*currenti*, 6) has been metamorphosed into an almost tragic figure, and that very metamorphosis expresses the changing terms of the relation between slave and master. What is caught by this poem is the drama of the developing relation between master and slave; of the hopes and needs of both parties, in this case cruelly cut off when they were on the point of realization. If one had to sum up the affect of this inscription, the formulation of Dupont (1992) will do quite well: "A special sentiment that was neither friendship nor

---

[4] Cf. Alexis 263K–A and Plautus *Poenulus* 522–3; also Cicero *De Officiis* 1.131.

[5] Guardi (1974).

love but a sort of grateful compassion bound citizens to their slaves" (58). But any formulation that tries to fix the affect will miss the dynamism of the relationship and the way it strains against its own limits.

It is quite possible that this epitaph from Cologne was read by the fourth-century writer Ausonius and struck him enough to influence his own poem, "In Notarium" (*Ephemeris* 7), in which case we would have the very unusual phenomenon of an inscription influencing a literary work, rather than vice versa.[6] Ausonius's emphasis is rather different, and for him the astonishing skill of the boy, which seems to anticipate the master's very thoughts, is a little disturbing:

> quis quaeso, quis me prodidit?
> quis ista iam dixit tibi,
> quae cogitabam dicere?
> quae furta corde in intimo
> exercet ales dextera?
> quis ordo rerum tam novus,
> veniat in aures ut tuas
> quod lingua nondum absolverit?   (22–9)

> Tell me, who is it who betrayed me?
> Who told you everything
> I had in mind to say?
> What thefts from deep in my heart
> does your winged right hand perform?
> What is this novel state of affairs,
> that what my tongue has not yet formed
> should reach your ears?

The regret of the inscription's master that he will not have anyone with whom to share his secrets has turned into a suspicion of the mind-reader, and the stenographer's winged hand has become the thieving hand of the stereotypical troublesome slave.[7] Ausonius raises the specter of an *ordo novus* in which slave anticipates master, but quickly dispels it by concluding that this skill comes not from *doctrina*, nor even from a swift hand, but rather from nature and from god:

---

[6] Green (1991), 261.
[7] Bradley (1994), 115–16; a good example is Pliny *NH* 33, 26–7.

natura munus hoc tibi
deusque donum tradidit
quae loquerer ut scires prius
idemque velles quod volo.   (33–6)

Nature, and god
gave this gift to you
to anticipate what I'll say
and for my wish to be yours.

Here is a more reassuring interpretation of the slave-stenographer's anticipation of his master, and it suggests that this poem is not so much about the skill of a swift hand as about the intimate knowledge that any slave may have of his master. The slightly facetious tone of Ausonius' wonder at the stenographer's mind-reading papers over a deeper anxiety. Only if the slave's knowledge of the master is restricted to the latter's needs is it reassuring, and the poem reaches closure when an interpretation of this puzzling and potentially disturbing ability of the slave is found that is compatible with his subordination. The final line depends on a pun on the word *volo*, both "mean" and "wish": anticipation of the master's thoughts becomes accordance with his wishes.

Ausonius wrote two poems about another stenographer, Pergamus, as incompetent as his fellow was impressive (*Epigrams* 16 and 17). Pergamus tried to run away, but he was as slow a runner as he was a writer, and ended up with a tattoo on his brow (a common punishment for runaways).[8] In these poems, Ausonius makes nasty fun of the slave's punishment, joking that his brow receives the letters that his right hand missed, and that he should either inscribe the hand that won't run or weigh down his fugitive legs with irons; as it is, he's punishing the wrong part of his body. So much for Christianity's humanitarian effect on ancient slavery![9] It is tempting to read into this comic overkill a reassertion of power over a slave for whose abilities his master feels a slightly disturbing wonder.

As we will see, it is a recurring paradox of domestic slavery that in order to serve the master properly the slave must have knowledge and abilities that contradict his official status. As Martial puts it in a more down-to-earth and decidedly unthreatening context:

[8] Jones (1987).
[9] On the vexed question of the effect of Christianity on slavery, see de Ste Croix (1981), 418–25, Lane Fox (1986), 295–9 and Garnsey (1997), 102–4.

> Non satis est ars sola coco: servire palatum
>   nolo: cocus domini debet habere gulam.   (14.220)

Art alone is not enough for a cook: I would not have his palate that of a slave; a cook ought to possess the taste of his master.

It is part of the job of Martial's cook to develop a master's palate, but other slaves might pick up their masters' sensibilities by the mere fact of cohabitation, just as Aristotle claimed that slaves would assimilate their masters' virtue (see above, p. 7). If the master is a satirist or philosopher, there is rich potential for irony when the slave starts to ape his master. This is what happens in Horace *Satires* 2.7, where the satirist's slave, Davus, decides that he has been a listener too long, and launches into his own diatribe against his master based on the Stoic paradox that every fool is a slave.[10]

It is the thrust of Davus' philosophical diatribe that "slavery" is something that affects us all to some degree or other, but the question is, "Who is the more slave, me or you?" Apparently, Davus has learnt his philosophy from the horse's mouth, or as near to that as a slave can get: "Stay your hand and control your temper," he says to his fuming master, "while I expound what Crispinus' doorman told me" (44–5). What Davus claims he has learnt from the philosopher's slave is that the master who pursues adulterous affairs, ending up in the most undignified and dangerous positions, is more of a slave than the slave himself, who satisfies his physical lust in the most expedient fashion.[11] Perhaps we are meant to smile at the lowly source of this second-hand Stoicism, but if the doorman is not the most reliable of philosophers, he is precisely the person who would be in a position to observe the comic comings and goings of upper-class love. The door who is the speaker of Catullus 67, garrulous as the *ianitor* himself, tells us a host of juicy secrets about his present and previous "masters." So Crispinus' doorman may be a good authority for what Davus has to say after all.

Horace, Davus contends, is himself the true slave, but that is a perception available to Davus because he is himself a real slave. The slave as metaphor is overlaid by the slave as metonym: the part of the master that

[10] Compare Persius 5.73–91, where the speaker addresses a newly emancipated slave whom he claims is not truly (ethically) free – an inversion of this poem.

[11] Horace *Satires* 1.2 makes this same contrast, with the satirist taking the position that Davus appropriates here.

is his self-consciousness, even conscience. If it is comforting for Horace the master to think of slavery as a moral state which he must guard himself from falling into, it is less so to acknowledge that slavery is a form of knowledge, providing a privileged position from which the master is observed.

Davus' main exhibit is the Horace who, having no dinner invitations, protests that simple dining is more to his taste; but should Maecenas extend a last minute invitation, the same Horace shouts at the slaves to get ready:

> iusserit ad se
> Maecenas serum sub lumina prima venire
> convivam: "nemone oleum feret ocius? Ecquis
> audit?" cum magno blateras clamore fugisque ...   (32–5)

> But suppose Maecenas
> invites you, a last minute guest, just when it's getting dark:
> "Won't someone bring me the oil, and fast? Is anyone
> listening?" You bawl at the top of your voice, and rush off.

The master's "is anyone listening" is answered ironically by the opening words of the poem:

> iamdudum ausculto et cupiens tibi dicere servus
> pauca reformido.   (1–2)

> I've been listening for a while now and, wanting to say
> a few words to you, as a slave I dare not.

Yes, there is someone listening. All the time. And that is the problem. As Samuel Johnson put it, "The danger of betraying our weakness to our servants, and the impossibility of concealing it from them, may be justly considered as one motive to live a regular and irreproachable life."[12] The number of *The Rambler* from which this passage comes (68) deals with the subject of private virtue on which, Johnson claims, it is the servant who has the authoritative perspective. He quotes as his epigraph Juvenal's "one must live an upright life, for many reasons, but mostly so that you can despise the tongue of the slave" (*vivendum recte, cum propter*

---

[12] Quoted by Robbins (1986), 100.

plurima, tunc est / idcirco ut possis linguam contemnere servi, 9.118–19), but Juvenal, unlike Johnson, is being sarcastic. It is doubtful whether any Roman master would have felt pressure to maintain appearances in front of the slaves, though Hopkins (1993) is surely right when he suggests that part of the reason why slaves were called "refuse" (*katharma*) and the like was that the free felt the need to cast back onto the slave the compromising qualities that slaves were in a position to observe in their masters (22–3). Furthermore, the very silence of the attendant slave prompts the master to imagine what he might be thinking, and to supply what he fears the slave has noticed, which is why Davus the slave can be read as a voice in Horace's head – the voice of conscience.

Horace allows Davus to speak because it is the festival of the *Saturnalia*, a time of freedom from restraints, especially for slaves, who were allowed various symbolic liberties. During the *Saturnalia*, slaves dined with their masters and, according to some accounts, masters waited upon their slaves.[13] Davus avails himself of the occasion to speak freely, without fear of his master's retribution.

> "iamdudum ausculto et cupiens tibi dicere servus
> pauca reformido." Davusne? "ita, Davus, amicum
> mancipium domino et frugi quod sit satis, hoc est
> ut vitale putes." age, libertate Decembri,
> quando ita maiores voluerunt, utere; narra.

> "I've been listening for a while now and, wanting to say
> a few words to you, as a slave I dare not." Is that Davus? "The same,
> a slave well-disposed to his master and honest enough, though not
> too good to live." Go on, then, use the license December allows,
> since our ancestors wanted it that way. Speak up.

The opening words anticipate the debut of Juvenal's satirist, speaking up finally because he can hold it in no longer: "Am I always to be a mere listener, and shall I never talk back? (*semper ego auditor tantum, numquamne reponam*? 1.1) This anticipation reminds us that, like the satirist who has been forced to listen to bad poets reciting, Davus speaks from the position of the reader, who has been listening now for a long time,

[13] On the *Saturnalia*, see Bradley (1987), 40–5, Versnel (1993), 150–63 and D'Arms (1991), 176.

though his status consigns him to silence. Horace's reaction to Davus' first words ("Is that Davus?") is the incredulous question of someone who thinks he has heard a statue speak. For the satirist, that statue is the reader, just as for the master it is the slave. In fact, there is always a potential satirist present, listening and observing, when someone, even a satirist, takes to speech; Horace himself begins his first book of *Satires* by castigating those who make pronouncements of the type "Happy the x, who doesn't have my problems."[14] There could be no better figure for the infinitely regressive position of the satirist than the slave, unnoticed and waiting to have his say, even if in this case the uncomfortable similarity between the satirist and the slave is muted by the fact that Davus is graciously granted the license to speak by his master (which may tell us something about the function of the *Saturnalia*).

Davus the listening slave appropriates, or is lent, certain stances that are typical of the satirist. But his name alludes to a figure from another genre, the clever slave of comedy, to whose paradoxical status he refers when he describes himself as *amicum mancipium domino*, both chattel and friend. After his preamble, Horace breaks in like the master in a comedy: "Won't you tell me (preferably sometime today) where all this garbage is going, gallowsbird?" (21–2),[15] and throughout Davus' speech he seethes with comic rage; violence hovers on the horizon (43–4) and finally breaks out in a barrage of threats at the end of the poem. This crossing of satire with comedy gives another dimension to the sexual accusations of Davus, for when he contrasts his own easily satisfied sexual desires to Horace's adulterous passions he not only speaks as the satiric moralist but he also conjures up, and refuses, the position of the comic slave who assists his young master in his amours, all the while mocking his witless besottedness.[16] Like Mozart's Leporello, Davus refuses to serve any more.

Inserting his master into a stock scene from the adultery mime,[17] in which the "slavish" lover, stripped of his equestrian insignia and dressed as a slave, is smuggled into his mistress's house, Davus asks the question "Aren't you what you pretend to be?" (*non es quod simulas*? 56). The play

---

[14] Oliensis (1998), 51–63 shows how the satirists of Book 2 satirize the satirists of Book 1.

[15] Horace has himself become the imaginary figure who interrupts the satirist at *Satires* 1.2.23, asking "*quo res haec pertinet*?"

[16] A point made by Bernstein (1992), 46.   [17] Muecke (1993), 221.

of masks goes deeper than Davus supposes, as we are indirectly reminded when Davus accuses Horace of being a puppet manipulated by foreign strings (82): the figure could just as well be applied to Davus who is, after all, himself Horace's creation. But if Horace the satirist impersonates his slave to voice (apparently unfair) criticisms of himself (72–3), might not Horace nevertheless be what he "pretends" to be?[18] Even if he is not the stereotypical servile adulterer conjured up by Davus, is he not the doctrinaire moralist who makes sweeping and generic accusations of people he doesn't really know; in other words, is he not the Davus against whom he protests? Muecke (1993) puts this well, "On the one hand, the gap between the preacher and what he preaches [e.g between Horace the "adulterer" and Horace the satirist of *Satires* 1.2], admittedly exaggerated, shows the difficulty of living according to a consistent set of principles. On the other, as we protest against Davus that our Horace is not like that, we are put in the position of defending the satiric victim in general against doctrinaire moralising" (213). The slave here is the imagined critical voice that, given its head, refuses to "serve" its limited purpose and proceeds to unravel the master's project.

Davus' final shot is a fairly standard satirical accusation:

> adde quod idem
> non horam tecum esse potes, non otia recte
> ponere, teque ipsum vitas fugitivus et erro,
> iam vino quaerens, iam somno fallere curam. (111–14)

> And into the bargain
> you can't be with yourself an hour, nor use your leisure
> properly, but flee yourself like a runaway or truant,
> looking to baffle care with wine or with sleep.

Being able to "be with oneself" here is being able to confront one's mental demons (*cura*), and is paradoxically figured as a relation between two people. The Horace who avoids himself is like the slave who either runs away (*fugitivus*) or goes AWOL (*erro*), an analogy supported by the use of *ipse*, a common expression for "the master."[19] Davus adopts the philo-

---

[18] Bernstein (46) argues that Horace is trying to make himself innocent by association of the more worrying accusation of servility.

[19] On the *erro* (a dilatory slave, slow to return to the household), see Bradley (1990), 144.

sophical *topos* of the divided soul, in which the degenerate, recalcitrant or acrasic self is figured as the slave, a *topos* which implied that slavery was in the interests of the slave as well as the master (see chapters 4 and 5). As long as the slave is thought of as a person dependent on the master, not only materially but in his very being, then the runaway is one who loses, rather than reclaims himself. But, look at the situation from the point of view of the enslaved, or turn the philosophical issue into one of emancipation or autarchy, rather than ataraxy, and the runaway slave takes on a different aspect. Epictetus, himself an ex-slave, holds up the runaway as the example of one who trusts in himself rather than externals (*Dis.* 9.2); in other words, he gives the figure the opposite significance to what it has for Horace's Davus, who seems to voice the attitude of the masters. But there may be an unruliness to Davus' use of this figure if we accept that the slave is the very embodiment of the fact that the master cannot be alone for a moment. One of the things slaves were for, as Dupont (1992) remarks, was simply to be there: Statius ("he who waits") was a common name for a slave (58). If it seems paradoxical to say that the Horace who cannot be with himself is like a runaway slave, the runaway slave is nevertheless an appropriate figure to conjure up when accusing a master of being incapable of facing himself. To turn the *fugitivus* into the figure of the imperfect man who can't bear to be on his own is both to hide and to reveal the fact that the attendant slave protects the master from ever being alone.

The poem ends with Horace reaching not for the whip, but for a stone (as though Davus were a dog) and for arrows (as though Horace were a god):[20]

> unde mihi lapidem? 'quorsum est opus?' unde sagittas?
> 'aut insanit homo aut versus facit.' ocius hinc te
> ni rapis, accedes opera agro nona Sabino.   (116-18)

> Someone give me a stone. 'What for?' Give me arrows.
> 'The man's either insane or he's versifying.' Get out
> or you'll find yourself the ninth hand on my Sabine farm.

Calling Davus a dog assimilates the omnipresent slave, polar opposite to the *fugitivus*, to the "dark companion" (*comes atra*, 115) that pursues the

---

[20] Muecke (1993), 226.

haunted master. Davus' persistent presence can stand for the very *cura* that Horace seeks hopelessly to avoid. But if the slave is a dog to the master, the master is a god to the slave: asking for his arrows, Horace poses as the god Apollo. "The man's either mad, or he's versifying (*versus facit*, 117)," Davus retorts, in a brilliant deflation of his master's grandiloquence, and in the process he brings the poem full-circle, *versus* being an anagram of *servus* in the first line of the poem. But "Horace" is not so subtle, and he ends the interchange with a threat straight out of comedy: if Davus doesn't behave himself he'll be sent to work on the country estate. There the poem ends.

In comedy, the slave is not actually relegated to the country, for all his master's threats.[21] Comedy's interchanges between clever slave and exasperated master, to which Horace's poem alludes, remind us that it is part of the ideology of slave literature that master and slave are locked in an antagonistic relationship that neither can do without. In Plautine comedy the underlying enmity is acknowledged but rendered comically compulsive. Sagaristio, one of the slaves in Plautus' *Persa*, compares the symbiotic relationship between master and slave to an itch:

ego nec lubenter servio neque satis sum ero ex sententia,
sed quasi lippo oculo me erus meus manum apstinere hau quit tamen,
quin me imperet, quin me suis negotiis praefulciat.   (10–12)

I'm not a willing slave, nor much to my master's taste,
but like an itchy eye my master can't keep his hand off me,
he orders me about and uses me to shore up his affairs.

When he complains that his master can't keep his hands off him we expect Sagaristio to follow up with some grim joke about punishment, but instead he complains of being ordered about, which in turn translates into having to act as the prop of his master's affairs. Whose hand is on whom? The slave is as essential as an eye and as irritating and inconsequential as an itch, and this paradoxical form of intimacy results in a paradoxical response, just as the hand that rubs the eye only aggravates the symptoms it is trying to alleviate.[22] Some twenty lines later, Sagaristio uses the figure of the itch again, this time supplying the flogging joke that we expected in the earlier passage. When a fellow slave invites him over to dine regally

---

[21] Tyndarus, in the *Captivi*, being the exception that proves the rule.
[22] Compare *Bacchides* 913–15.

while his master is away, Sagaristio replies "God, my shoulders itch on hearing you say that" (*Vah, iam scapulae pruriunt, qui te istaec audivi loqui*, 32). The slave is the master's itch and the master the slave's. *Prurire* (itch) is a verb that is also used for sexual desire, more particularly, the desire of the pathic, so Sagaristio's words express the slave's *desire* to transgress as well as his fear of punishment. Between them, these images of the master's inflamed eye and the servant's itchy back express the comic symbiosis of master and slave that is central to the economy of Plautine comedy, a symbiosis expressed in more condensed form by the following exchange from *Epidicus*: "I'm in love" says the master; "My shoulders feel it" answers the slave (66). The repetition of this stereotype reassures the audience that, beneath the gross inequity of the relationship, and in spite of the resentment of the slave, master and slave are bound together by a division of labor, a comic complementarity. "What's up?" asks the master; "You're in love and I'm hungry" comes the answer (*Casina*, 724–5; cf. 801ff.).

In Plautus, there are practical reasons why the master needs the slave: high-class love makes you lose your wits as well as your dignity and, like Wodehouse's Wooster, the young master is not overendowed with wits in the first place. The clever slave is there to help his young master outmanoeuvre the father, pimp or braggart soldier who stands between him and the consummation of his desires. In the process, the scheming slave becomes (in his own eyes, at any rate) a general, a politician or even a playwright, turning the tables on his master.[23] There is a social reality shadowing this farce, the reality of the "clever, talented, educated slave occupying a position of responsibility, who has a realistic prospect of freedom and the constant image before his or her eyes of other slaves who had achieved freedom."[24] Though the literary motif of the clever, scheming slave comes from Greek New Comedy (see Menander's *Aspis* and *Dis Exapaton*), it takes on new meaning in adaptations of Greek plays at Rome, where scheming and deceit are "Greek" characteristics.[25] It is significant, for instance, that Greek words and phrases in Plautus are usually spoken by slaves, and that they are likely to be Plautine additions rather than echoes of his Greek sources.[26]

[23] Fraenkel (1960), 223–31 and Segal (1987), 143–54.   [24] Hopkins (1993), 6.

[25] Fraenkel (1960), 223–41 argues that Plautus significantly increased the role of the slave. Dumont (1987), 498–9, puts the case against Fraenkel. For ancient references to the clever slave in New Comedy, see Spranger (1961), 37, n.1.

[26] Shipp (1953).

Just as the desire of the enamored master finds its lower equivalent in the hunger of the slave, and the former's amatory torment in the latter's tortured back, so in other contexts the slave's street savvy provides a cut-price version of the sagacity of his masters. In Terence, two delicious scenes revolve around the slave's parody of the conventional wisdom of the free: Syrus mockingly adapts Demea's pompous exposition of his principles of education to his own precepts on the proper way to prepare fish (*Adelphoe* 412–32) and Geta recasts the philosophical Demipho's remarks on the wisdom of being prepared for the worst to reflect his own mental preparation for a beating (*Phormio* 239–251). But such scenes are most characteristic of another literary pair, namely the philosopher and the slave, and it is worth dwelling on them for a moment.

On the face of it, the slave is the polar opposite of the philosopher, body to the latter's mind. But the slave, like the philosopher, is an out-sider, and both, in their different ways, have knowledge of underlying causes. The affinity of slave and philosopher is bolstered by the fact that many philosophers, especially of the Cynic persuasion, had been, or were reputed to have been, slaves.[27] The most extended representation of this comic pair is the *Life of Aesop*, an anonymous biography of the legen-dary fabulist which seems to have accreted a collection of popular stories about slaves and masters, and was written down in its present form in the early Empire.[28] Like Horace and Davus on the *Saturnalia*, Aesop and his master Xanthos are a reversible pair, Xanthos being a common name for a slave and Aesop a figure who has much in common with Socrates. Aesop is every bit as ugly as the snub-nosed philosopher; he harries pro-fessional intellectuals, and finally he dies at the hands of citizens he has insulted. Where the slave-satirist sees the foibles and inconsistencies of humanity by virtue of his position as attendant, the slave-philosopher knows how the world works through being at the bottom of the ladder. One of the students dining at Xanthos' house proposes the question "What will cause great disturbance among men?" To which Aesop, stand-ing behind his master, replies "If the dead arise and ask for the return of

---

[27] Patterson (1991), 184.

[28] Text in Perry (1952); I quote from *Vita* G. The ancient testimonia on Aesop, from Herodotus on, are collected in Perry, 211–41. See Holzberg (1993), 17–18 for a brief discussion of Aesop's historicity, and 80–4 on the manuscripts of the *Vita*. Hopkins (1993) is a splendid study of this work and of what it tells us about slavery.

their property" (47). If slavery is social death, as Patterson (1982) has argued, then Aesop speaks as one of those dead who threaten to reclaim their rights. Another student asks "Why is it that a sheep being led to the slaughter doesn't cry out but a pig squeals loudly?" (48) Only Aesop can come up with an answer: because the sheep knows it can be sheared or milked, whereas the pig knows it has only its meat to offer. Other examples of Aesopian wisdom exhibit the same understanding from below (e.g. 49–50).

Like Davus lecturing Horace, Aesop repeatedly finds opportunities to teach his master, the professor, a lesson about the proper way to give orders. Xanthos, in turn, looks for excuses to beat his slave. Together they perform a dance. At one point, Xanthos, frustrated by Aesop's ingenious misunderstanding of his instructions, tells him to do nothing more or less than he is instructed. Naturally, this only leads to further "misunderstandings" as Aesop takes his master exactly at his word; when Xanthos tells Aesop "Take the oil flask in your hands, and the towels, and let's go to the baths," Aesop brings the flask but not the oil (38), and so on.[29] Aesop can prove he has "obeyed" Xanthos using the same kind of demonstrations the philosopher uses with his pupils, and he adds "you shouldn't have been so precise in laying down the law, and I would have served you properly. The way you decreed the law to me will be useful to you, for it will teach you not to make mistakes in the classroom. Statements that include or exclude too much are no small mistakes" (43). Not only does Aesop have a version of his master's theoretical knowledge, but this knowledge derives from a practical experience of one of the great contradictions of slavery, identified by Hopkins (1993) in his study of this work. We could rephrase it as follows: on the one hand the master wants the slave to be an automaton who is nothing more than an extension of his will, but on the other hand he needs the slave to take some initiative if he is to be properly served.

For another master who wants nothing of the slave's initiative, we can turn to what looks like a much more straightforward view of the relationship between master and slave, namely Horace, *Odes* 1.38, in which the poet addresses an excessively officious slave. Here, more conventionally, it is the master, not the slave, who has a lesson to teach.

---

[29] On this episode, see Hopkins (1993), 18–19, who cites a very similar anecdote about M. Pupius Piso, consul of 61 BCE.

Persicos odi, puer, apparatus,
displicent nexae philyra coronae:
mitte sectari, rosa quo locorum
      sera moretur.
simplici myrto nihil allabores
sedulus curo: neque te ministrum
dedecet myrtus neque me sub arta
      vite bibentem.

Boy, I hate those Persian preparations:
crowns woven with baste displease me;
don't bother to look for where
      the late rose lingers.
I care nothing that you labour to improve
plain myrtle: myrtle's not unsuitable
for you who serve, nor for me, drinking
      under the thick vine.[30]

Horace goes further than Xanthos and denies the whole structure of command on which the relationship is built. After telling the slave in some detail what he doesn't want, he issues no order, and the peremptory tone fades into the final double negative (*neque . . . dedecet*, 6–7). For the slave-owner, all pleasures are accompanied by imperatives, but the persona of this poem has no orders to give, and the imperatives try to negate the fact that the slave's work comes between the master and his pleasure. In fact, Horace seeks to substitute the pleasures of textuality for the pleasure that is mediated, and alienated, by the slave. Hegel pointed out, in his discussion of the relation between master and slave at the beginning of the *Phenomenology,* that the master relates to the material world solely as consumer, whereas the slave transforms it with his work.[31] Horace's poem, itself a thing made, rebels against this division. Although this is not a dramatic work, and contains no dialogue, there is nevertheless an interesting dialectic being played out between the work of the slave and the work of the poet. Here, far from the slave triumphing by virtue of his parodic version of the master's own capacities, it is the master who appropriates and transforms the work of the slave.

---

[30] Excellent discussion of this poem in Lowrie (1997), 164–75. See also Fitzgerald (1989).   [31] Hegel (1977), 115–18.

Waving away the preparations of the slave, Horace denies both the luxury and the servility that are conjured up by the word *Persicos*. Since the poem closes the first book of Horace's *Odes*, and follows a grand, public poem (the "Cleopatra" Ode), we are teased with the possibility that there is a programmatic aspect to the poem. Is it a vindication of the simple style? If so, this highly wrought and jewelled poem, whose protestations of easy carelessness are belied by the obvious care that has been taken by the poet, turns the poet into a higher-level version of the officious slave. We might invoke the language of Hegel to say that the work of the slave is *aufgehoben*: removed, preserved and also, in the process, lifted to a higher plane. Take the second line of the poem, *displicent nexae philyra coronae*: juxtaposed to *nexae*, *displicent* becomes a pun (and an oxymoron) as the *-plic-* that is the compounded form of *placeo* metamorphoses into the *-plic-* of *plico* (fold): 'the woven chains unfold'. This wordplay is reinforced by *simplici* in the same position of the first line of the next stanza. The careful effect of textuality emerges from the rejection of a more literal textuality (wovenness) as the slave is told not to weave an elaborate crown – plain myrtle will do fine. Even here the double negative, *neque dedecet*, is a circumlocution that is complicit with the very elaboration it rejects. We could say that the work of the poet and the elaboration of his poem become visible at the very point where the work of the slave is being undone (*dis-plic*).

A similar effect occurs at the beginning of the second stanza, where it is not clear whether we should translate *sedulus* with *allabores* ("I care nothing that you should labor to improve on plain myrtle") or with *curo* ("I carefully see to it that you do not labor to improve . . .") – *nihil curo* or *sedulus curo*? In my translation I have gone for the first alternative, which fits the casual voice of the master's persona, and the trajectory from the stronger expressions of the first stanza's *odi* to the weaker *neque dedecet* with which the poem ends. But the word order and the enjambement make it more natural to read *sedulus curo*. Again, the poem as text conflicts with the poem as fictional utterance of its persona, and the master's casual indifference to the slave's work becomes the poet's careful prevention (getting there first). Finally, the placement of the words '*sera moretur*' at the end of the first stanza, filling the stanza's shorter line, lovingly prolongs the separate lingering of the late rose that the master tells the slave not to search out. Far from the rose being a matter of indifference to the master, it would seem that it is being *preserved* from the officious ministrations of the slave in this alternative, textual incarnation.

When the master pictures himself and the boy, crowned with plain myrtle, they are beneath "a thick vine" (*arta vite*), the slave serving and the master drinking.[32] This thick vine is not only an efficient sunshade but also the tightly woven text, and the sense of intricacy and tautness that the word *arta* conveys in this connection works in counterpoint to the casual picture that is being conjured up. We are left with a poised balance between closure and openness in the final picture of the master, whose *sprezzatura* is displayed against the laborious preparations of the slave.

Horace's slave, unlike the stenographer Xanthias with whom we started, has clearly not read his master's mind, nor are his tastes those of his master, like Martial's cook. And yet it is through the quarrel with the person who is most intimately implicated in the poet's pleasure that the textual work and pleasure of the Horatian poem is realized. Another Horatian slave who is betraying his master's principles appears in the envoi to the first book of Horace's *Epistles* (*Ep.*1.20), addressed to the finished opus as though it were a young and recently manumitted slave, eager to display himself to a broader public and see something of the world.[33] The published book (*liber*) is a free (*liber*) slave, a pun echoed by Ovid in *Tristia* 1.1 (1–2, 15–16, 57–8), where, ironically, it is the book that is free (to go to Rome) while the master is not.[34] Horace the master warns his book/slave of the fickle public and of the sordid life that awaits him once his bloom has worn off. As the finished book, the slave both is and isn't an extension of the master, who seems to be questioning the very impulse that brought him to publish the book. The boy's ambition is misguided, and yet it echoes Horace's: he is instructed to tell the world that Horace, the freedman's son, "spread wings too wide for his nest" (20–1). Here, the poet's internal quarrel with himself through the medium of the slave bears a relation to the Davus *Satire*.[35]

---

[32] West (1995), 193 argues that the myrtle indicates an erotic relationship between master and slave.   [33] On this poem, see Oliensis (1995) who compares *Sat.*1.10.92.

[34] Hinds (1985), 13–14 and 29, n.2.

[35] *Epode* 4, a savage attack on a freedman who has become *tribunus militum* (like Horace himself, *Satires* 1.6.45ff.), begins "you and I are as inimical to each other as wolves and lambs." Is Horace "making faces at the mirror"? See Oliensis (1998), 66–8. If Williams (1995) is right that Horace's identification of himself as a freedman's son is exaggerated, then the "reality" that might be thought to underlie Horace's servile tropes may itself be one of them.

We will return to Horace in chapter 3, apropos an elaborate simile in which the poet casts himself as both slave and slave-dealer in relation to a friend to whom he has promised a poem that has not been forthcoming (*Epistles* 2.2.1–25). But a comparison of *Odes* 1.38 with a poem like *Odes* 3.29 uncovers another sense in which Horace the poet overlaps with the slave. In 3.29 Maecenas is called away from the city with its smoke, wealth and noise, to the retreat where Horace has readied for him wine, roses and a pillow for his head. The poet now plays the role of the ministering *puer* to his great friend. But the framework has changed: here it is Maecenas, not the slave, who is the laborious one, preoccupied with concerns about the state (25–8); Horace's plain fare and humble dwelling may serve to unknit the furrowed brow (*sollicitam explicuere frontem*, 16) of Maecenas just as Horace undid the laborious preparations of the boy in 1.38. Maecenas is invited to reclaim himself, as his own master (*potens sui*, 41), from his servitude to the Roman people.[36]

In these poems, Horace plays variations on the theme of slavery, locating himself in different or multiple positions within the unit of slave and master, which itself admits of a variety of determinations. As poet, he is concerned both with pleasure, which he purveys to those more laborious than himself, and with a certain kind of technique. The figure of the slave allows him to place himself by means of differentiations and redistributions within the master/slave relationship. What is striking in these usages is the way slave and master interpenetrate, extend each other, or exchange positions, a feature of the symbiotic relation between master and slave in all of the material that I have cited in this chapter.

---

[36] See Martin (1990), chapter 3, "The Enslaved Leader" on this figure (compare Publilius Syrus 519 Duff).

Punishment: license, (self-) control and fantasy

In Latin there is an active verb that means "to be beaten" (*vapulo*), a verb that occurs frequently in Plautus – being beaten is one of the most important things that literary slaves do. Listing the tasks required of a maid, Demipho in Plautus' *Mercator* comes up with the following:

> nihil opus nobis ancilla nisi quae texat, quae molat,
> lignum caedat, pensum faciat, aedis verrat, vapulet. (396–7)[1]

> We have no need of a maid, except one to weave, grind,
> cut wood, do her spinning, sweep the house, be beaten.

The second line takes the maid smoothly from chopping wood to being beaten, as though she were herself absorbed into the world of things that she pounds, sweeps and generally works on, a world that takes its revenge on her in a sudden reversal that depends on the active form of *vapulo*. Martial displays a similarly cold humor in answer to a certain Rusticus, who has accused him of cruelty and gluttony because he beats the chef on account of a poor meal:

> si levis ista tibi flagrorum causa videtur,
> ex qua vis causa vapulet ergo cocus? (8.23.3–4)

> If that seems a trivial offense for the whip,
> for what reason *would* you have me beat the cook?

---

[1] Cf. *Mercator*, 416.

If the slave, in slaveholder ideology, is the being that is beaten, and the whip the primary symbol of the master's power over the slave,[2] it is one of the most important marks of the free man that his body is immune to punishment; for a free man, to be stripped and beaten publicly is to suffer a massive blow to his honor and a total deprivation of personal dignity.[3] As one of Plautus' slave characters says to his master, "Freedom is a cloak over your back" (*Mostellaria* 991), a point made from another angle in the sole fragment of Plautus' lost *Faeneratrix*, where a newly emancipated slave says "Welcome freedom, go to hell/be beaten (*vapula*) Papiria [the ex-slave's mistress]." A slave in Terence (*Heautontimorumenos* 356) uses a common play on words to distinguish the punishment he risks as a slave from the reprimand that the young man may incur: "for you there will be words (*verba*), for this man [me] there will be a beating (*verbera*)."[4]

Plautine comedy is riddled with references to beating, though, as Erich Segal pointed out in a classic study (1987), the presiding Saturnalian spirit ensures that beating, constantly threatened, is always postponed. At the end of *Pseudolus*, the title character reassures his outwitted master, fuming with desire for revenge, with the words "Why threaten me? I have a back" (1325). Simo, who has challenged Pseudolus to outwit him, and lost, is constrained by the terms of his bet for the duration of the play, but after it has ended normal relations will resume. Such reminders of the slave's vulnerability, as inescapable a fact as his anatomy, must have been reassuring to the slave-owning audience that had entertained solidarity with the cheeky slave for the duration of the play. The interchange between Simo and his slave draws our attention to two contradictory features of the literature of slavery: first, the constant reminders that it is the slave's lot to be beaten, and second, the repeated scenes in which the master is cheated of the satisfaction of beating his slave. Of course, there is nothing to stop Simo from beating his slave, but that would spoil the fun, which depends on the temporary triumph of the powerless.

What is striking in the case of the literary pair, comic master and slave, is that the slave can hold the master to a kind of contract which the master implicitly acknowledges. In the *Life of Aesop* the drama of the relationship between Aesop and his master depends on the constant

---

[2] Finley (1980), 93. Compare Herodotus' story about the Scythians (4.1–4), discussed by Hunter (1992).   [3] Saller (1994), 135–50 and Aulus Gellius 10.3.

[4] Cf. Seneca *Ep.*47.19.

frustration of Xanthos' desire to have his slave beaten. Aesop manages
to draw his master into a game in which he repeatedly, but not quite con-
sistently, cheats his master of the right to beat him by proving that his dis-
obedience is in fact obedience. Again, there is nothing to stop Xanthos
from simply having Aesop beaten for insolence – that is his right as
master; but as someone who prides himself on his rationality, he is held
to an implicit agreement that works to his disadvantage: "Xanthos,
finding no pretext for beating Aesop, held his peace" (43).[5] Hopkins
remarks on the extraordinary fact that these tales assume that the reader
(or listener, with a slave reading aloud!) will side with the slave against the
master.[6] But this is not only a story about a slave and his master, it is also
a drama of the conflict between two different kinds of intelligence.
Xanthos' tolerance of Aesop's reasoning is comically absurd, and
perhaps assimilates him to the *scholasticus*, a stock comic figure who features in anecdotes about the impracticality and fatuousness of the pro-
fessional intellectual.[7] Part of the fun here is surely the ludicrous
consequence of Xanthos' impractical commitment to logic. The master
who lets his slave get away with this kind of behavior is like the proverbial philosopher who falls into the pit while looking at the sky, which
gives the audience an alibi for siding with the slave.

But it is not always the slave who has the upper hand in these confron-
tations; other anecdotes record failed attempts by slaves to use their
masters' philosophy against them, and these highlight the wit of the
masters rather than the cunning of the slaves. Diogenes Laertius (7.23)
relates that a slave of Zeno who was being whipped for stealing appealed
to Stoic philosophy by complaining that it was his fate ($\epsilon \H{\iota} \mu \alpha \rho \tau o$) to steal.
"Yes, and to be beaten too" was Zeno's reply. A similar story is told of
Plutarch (Aulus Gellius 1.26.5–7), whose slave remonstrated while being
beaten that his master had written a treatise "On Freedom from Anger".
Plutarch replied calmly, and with leisurely rhetorical amplification,
"What is it that makes you think I am angry? My tone of voice, my
expression, my colour. . . ?" After elaborating on this theme, he turned to
the man who was plying the lash and said: "In the meantime, while this
fellow and I are arguing, keep to your task (*hoc age*)." Plutarch's fulsome-

[5] As Hopkins (1993), 14 puts it "The master can beat the slave, cheat him of his promised freedom, but only at the cost of showing up his own moral inferiority."
[6] Hopkins (1993), 19. On *lectores*, see Starr (1991).   [7] Winkler (1985), 160–3.

ness prolongs the punishment, the master's ample rhetoric being accompanied by the cries of the slave. The man of intellect distinguishes himself from the man of the body and the passions by having an intermediary act out his anger for him; that intermediary was certainly himself a slave. Galen would have approved of the urbane Plutarch: he recommended avoiding unhealthy fits of anger by having others beat the slaves, and with the proper instruments, rather than striking out on the spur of the moment with whatever comes to hand, or indeed the hand itself (*Morb. An.*4).

Even Plato features in a beating-the-slave anecdote, this one in a treatise on anger of the kind to which Plutarch's slave appeals, Seneca's *De Ira* (3.12.5–7). On the point of angrily beating his slave, Plato suddenly checked himself, freezing in the position, "disgraceful (*deformem*) for a wise man," of one about to strike, hand upraised. When a puzzled Speusippus came across him in this pose, Plato explained that he was punishing an angry man. He asked Speusippus to take over, remarking "That slave should not be in the power of one who has no power over himself."

As we saw in the previous chapter, the structural relations between slave and philosopher are particularly rich. Stories about philosophers disciplining their slaves (or not) may oppose practical wisdom to theoretical, to the benefit of the former, or body to mind, with the philosopher retaining the advantage. Not only can the philosopher's self-control – the domination of his passions by his intellect – be *figured* by the master's control of his slave, but this self-control is best *tested* in dealings with slaves, since it is the presence of the slave that renders the master vulnerable to one of the most dangerous of emotions, anger.[8] Plutarch's *De Cohibenda Ira* and Seneca's *De Ira* reflect the centrality of this emotion to the philosophy of the passions. In fact, the very presence of slaves, omnipresent cushions between the master or mistress and a recalcitrant world, must have increased the temptation to indulge anger, especially with beings who were credited with no right to fair treatment. In this respect, the usual distinction between the pampered domestic slave and his maltreated rural counterpart breaks down, for the domestic slave is

---

[8] Aristotle has a revealing description of anger as listening to reason but not hearing it aright, like an overhasty slave who does not stay to hear the full instructions and bungles the job (*NE* 1149a9).

that much closer to the master's or mistress's moods. Juvenal paints a famously horrific picture of a cruel mistress taking out anger at her husband's coldness or dissatisfaction with her appearance on her slaves (6.474–96). Another Juvenalian wife, when her husband protests against her order that a slave be crucified (6.219ff.), arguing that there has been no hearing and that no delay is long when a man's life is at stake, replies "Lunatic, is a slave then a human? Suppose he's done nothing: this is what I want, this what I command, let my will serve as reason."[9] A more chilling, because less dramatic, reminder of the connection between slaves and anger comes from the enlightened Seneca (*Ep.*2.6), who warns Lucilius that immoderate anger begets madness, adding that anyone knows this who has an enemy or a slave. In the letter on slaves (*Ep.* 47), he urges Lucilius to remind himself, whenever he thinks of the license (*quantum liceat*) that he has over the slave, that his own master has the same license (*tantumdem licere*) over him. Slaves are really "fellow slaves" if we remember that fortune has the same license (*tantumdem licere*) over us both. The repetition of the verb *licere* is telling: slaves are beings with respect to whom one is allowed to indulge oneself.

Latin literature is studded with anecdotes of cruel and arbitrary punishment of slaves, a reflection not only of the fact that that this was a common occurrence, but also of the outrage that it could incur.[10] Some of this outrage was directed against the abuse of the slave, but for the most part it was the master's lack of self-control that was problematic: as Seneca's Plato has it, "That slave should not be in the power of one who has no power over himself." Because of what the free were allowed over slaves, behavior towards slaves was very revealing of one's self-control, or lack of it.

As one might expect, comedy is less concerned with these ethical issues. Jokes about the beating of slaves seem to have been deeply rooted in ancient comedy. Aristophanes, for instance, claims that he had done away with scenes in which slaves were thrown out of the house, lamenting, for the sole purpose that a colleague should mock them and ask "Wretch, what has happened to your skin? Could it be that the spiked whip has invaded your sides and ravaged your back ?" (*Peace*, 743–49) But even he is capable of building a scene around the beating of slaves (*Frogs* 631–73). However, nothing in the extant remains of ancient Greek comedy, old or

---

[9] Notice that her transgression against her gender role accompanies her transgression against the slave's humanity.   [10] Hopkins (1993), 7–10.

new, compares with the way the language of Plautus' comedies is satu-
rated with references to punishment. Crucifixion, fetters, the mill and,
above all, the whip provide the material for countless jokes. Comically
exaggerated threats, insults (*verbero*, *mastigia*, *crux*), and expressions of
fear pepper the dialogue. This phenomenon has been most recently
treated by Parker (1989) in a stimulating discussion which builds on
Segal's (1987) study of Plautus' "Saturnalian" comedy. Segal pointed out
that the pervasive threat of torture that hangs over the Plautine slave is
almost never realized. Punishment is suspended for the festive time of the
comedy during which a Saturnalian reversal of the normal hierarchy and
decorum prevails: today the *servus callidus* gets away with it (and everything goes), but tomorrow will be different, as was yesterday.[11] The slave,
according to Segal, is the incarnation of comedy's atmosphere of festive
license. Parker, citing Freud, starts from the premise that a great deal of
humor in general is a form of denial, or defusing of anxiety, and he
locates the relevant anxiety for comedy in the figure of the *servus callidus*.
According to Parker, the enormous influx of slaves from foreign wars
during Plautus' lifetime, together with the threat, and reality, of slave
revolts (four in Plautus' lifetime),[12] make the rebellious slave a potentially
terrifying specter. Plautus defuses this fear by constantly reminding his
audience of the ultimate power of the master over the cleverest slave.
Where for Segal punishment is threatened only to be suspended, so
marking the special festive time of the comedy, for Parker it is the slave's
unruly *calliditas* that is displayed only to be placed under the shadow of
punishment. These two interpretations are not necessarily mutually
exclusive. As Lott (1995) has shown for American Blackface, a genre that
has obvious affinities with Roman comedy, the audience may have
contradictory relations to its lowly heroes. He finds in Blackface minstrelsy a "dialectical flickering of racial insult and racial envy" (18).
Citing film theorists on the "destabilized structure of fascination," he
says: "The blackface phenomenon was virtually constituted by such slip-
pages, positives turning into negatives, selves into others, and back again.
There was in minstrelsy an unsteady but structured fluctuation between

[11] Segal (1987), 161; Plautine passages in Parker (1989), 238. For a later example of the
limits of Saturnalian impunity, see Martial 14.79.
[12] 217 BCE at Rome; 198 at Sestia; 196 in Etruria; 185 in Apulia. Parker (1989),
237–8.

fascination with (or dread of) 'blackness' and fearful ridicule of it" (124). Parker in fact recognizes this combination of fear and identification in Plautine comedy, for the second part of his article interprets the rebellious slave as a stand-in for the son, whose potential rebellion against the powerful Roman *paterfamilias* the slave enacts harmlessly, and is then excused the expected punishment. I will have more to say about this in chapter 4.

What is most striking about the obsessive references to beating in Plautine comedy is their linguistic exuberance. Pseudolus' laconic "I have a back" reminds us that one of the richest sources of linguistic play in the Plautine corpus is the slave's back. Appropriately enough, forms of the adjective *varius* crop up repeatedly in connection with floggings: the slave's back is "variegated" with the marks of the whip, just as the text continually finds new ways of figuring the immutable fact that the slave is the being who is beaten. Asked how he fares, the Plautine slave only has to say *varie* to raise a laugh.[13] In the prologue to the *Poenulus*, slaves are told to hand over their seats to the free, "or they'll be mottled here with the lash and with the rods at home" (*ne et hic varientur loris et virgis domi*, 26), the *variatio* of the slave's back being mirrored in the *variatio* of the chiastic pattern itself.

In many passages the whip makes an aesthetic object of the slave's variegated back: Campanian draperies, for instance, or Alexandrian rugs (*Pseudolus* 144–6); a painting (*Epidicus* 625–6); a surface daubed (*Asinaria*, 550) or covered with writing (*Pseudolus* 544–5). The slave is indeed the person who is beaten, but he is also a luxury object of display, and these aesthetic images are ironic reflections of the double status of the slave, both prized possession and being without honor.[14] Other ironic figures for beating similarly reflect ambiguities in the status of the slave. In the *Epidicus*, the eponymous slave responds to his master's threat of a beating with the words "without any outlay on my part a feast (*symbolae*) has been readied for my shoulders" (125). The excess of the punishment is ironically turned into a positive, a bounty bestowed on the slave.[15] But it is one of the facts of slavery often commented upon (by free writers)

---

[13] E.g. *Epidicus* 17–18 *qui varie valent, capreaginum hominum non placet mihi neque pantherinum genus.*

[14] By contrast, as Kathleen McCarthy points out to me *per litteras,* the good slave's unpunished back is a strictly utilitarian object: an unblemished hide from which you could make a wineskin (*Rudens* 755–7).

[15] Cf. *Rudens* 636, *ulmeam . . . virgidemiam.*

that the slave lives at the expense of the master.[16] Being a slave means both that the master is obliged to feed you at his expense (to preserve his investment) and that he is free to beat you at will. Later in *Epidicus* this figure is reversed, and the slave's back becomes a cornucopia that itself attracts parasites, the elm rods that "fleece" it (*ne ulmos parasitos faciat [sc. senex] si resciverit, quae usque attondeant*, 311).

Perhaps the most grotesque version of the slave's beaten back as riches is the little exchange between two slaves in *Asinaria*.

Leonida. etiam de tergo ducentas plagas praegnatis dabo.
Libanus. largitur peculium, omnem in tergo thensaurum gerit. (276–7)

Leonida. I will even give two hundred pregnant stripes from my back.
Libanus. He scatters his *peculium*, all his treasure's on his back.

The carrot and the stick of slavery, *peculium* and whip, are conflated in Libanus's retort, but Leonida's image of pregnancy suggests a context in which to think of all these positive images of whippings, and indeed of the text that teems with these endlessly varied images. In his book on Rabelais, Bakhtin shows that a feature of the carnival, and of the carnival text, is the imagining and display of a grotesque body, a body bursting its confines with a utopian generosity that conquers by inversion the fear of death.[17] If the grotesque body of the beaten slave served to conquer some fear, it is perhaps because witnessing the torment inflicted on another, even a slave, reminded the free of the vulnerability of their own bodies.[18] This is a possibility that Parker's interpretation of jokes about torture studiously avoids, even though the obvious application of his principle that jokes conceal (and defuse) fears and anxieties would be that jokes about the torture of slaves conceal and defuse anxieties stemming from that torture, not from the specter of the clever slave. Even if the free were themselves immune to corporal punishment, they too had bodies that could suffer. The regenerative grotesque body, copious in its variety, and symbiotic with the copious and teeming variety of the Plautine text itself, protected the audience from the disturbing reminder of the body's vulnerability provided by the beaten slave.

The image of the punished slave also conjures up a mirror world, where

---

[16] *Rudens* 181–3; *Persa* 471ff.; *Casina* 293.   [17] Bakhtin (1968), chapter 5.
[18] Compare the interesting anecdote of Ammonius having a slave beaten in order to reprimand his pupils (discussed below, p. 57).

the adjectives *bubulinus, ulmeus, ferreus* etc., alluding to the raw materials of instruments of punishment, are added to the vocabulary of citizenship and politics.[19] The majority of these figures are created by slave characters themselves, with an irony whose very excess parades their ability to appropriate the symbols of their enslavement and transform them into badges of honor mirroring those of the citizen.[20] Libanus' entrance in Act Three of *Asinaria* takes this to the limit (545–7), a speech of thanksgiving to all the wiles and trickeries by which he has triumphed, as though in a military campaign: relying on his shoulders and his forearms (*scapulorum confidentia, virtute ulnorum freti*), he has defeated all the instruments of torture ranged against him, and the "keenest painters, well acquainted with my back" (*inductores acerrumos gnarosque nostri tergi*). His speech culminates in a neat parallel between the brave soldier and the clever slave: "Who is more courageous than me when it comes to undergoing blows?" (557)[21] This appropriation of the language of honor by the one who is outside the society of those who claim honor neither reflects, nor is it meant to represent, a slave culture; it is entirely a fantasy of the free.[22] As McCarthy (forthcoming) argues, the slave is not required to maintain the physical dignity that is both the privilege and burden of free status, and can therefore be irreverent about his body in a way that might become an object of utopian longing for those who must always maintain the proper demeanor; the free must walk at a dignified pace but the excited slave is allowed, even expected, to run. The comic slave's proud use of the language of the whip, parodying the language of military and political honor, claims dishonor as a status that has its own privileges. The same is the case with moral dignity. Slaves were proverbially cowardly,[23] but the comic slave-hero positively vaunts his cowardice, giving birth to a long line of cowardly heroes that culminates in the Bob Hopes, Walter Mittys, and Woody Allens of modern American comedy. When Zero Mostel, in *A Funny Thing Happened on the Way to the Forum*, plays Pseudolus with impudent fear and trembling, the two ends of this tradition meet.

---

[19] E.g. *Epidicus* 5ff.; *Aulularia* 601; *Stichus* 663; *Persa* 22.

[20] This point is brilliantly made by McCarthy (forthcoming).

[21] On the simultaneously analogical and polar relation between slave and soldier (who was also subject to corporal punishment), see Walters (1997), 40.

[22] On slavery and honor, see Patterson (1982), 79–81.

[23] "Slaves as a class are utterly cowardly whenever there is any cause for fear" comments the narrator in Achilles Tatius' *Leucippe and Cleitophon* (7.10).

But the beaten slave does not always become a cowed, or cowardly, slave. Ovid warns his suspicious mistress, in a poem I will examine in the next chapter, that the beaten ass becomes less, not more, tractable (*Amores* 2.7.15–16). The slave's back is both the ultimate guarantor of the master's power over the slave ("why threaten me, I have a back") and the calloused surface where the slave's cleverness (*calliditas*) turns the master's violence back on himself. In *Pseudolus*, Ballio the pimp grumbles that his slaves are asses, so calloused are their backs with blows (*ita plagis costae callent*, 136; cf. *Asinaria* 419); beat them, and it's yourself you harm. These whip-worn (*flagitribae*, 137) slaves are devoted to the principle that whenever you get the opportunity you steal, drink, eat and flee. Ballio's vocabulary is particularly interesting here: *callent* juxtaposed to *flagitribae* amounts to a translingual pun, the Greek *trib-* that provides the suffix of *flagitribae* being the equivalent of the Latin *calleo,* as both derive their sense "cunning" from a primary meaning "rub" or "grow calloused". *Calleo* shares a root with *callidus*, the word that characterizes the clever (and intractable) slave (cf. Cicero, *N.D.* 3.25).[24] When Ballio alludes to the irony that the master who beats a slave ends up harming himself more than the slave, he brings out the connection between the two meanings of these roots, and the way that the metaphorical sense is derived from the literal.[25] The cleverness of the intractable slave's cunning is synonymous with the hardening of the skin, the imperviousness to punishment, that comes from continual beatings, themselves the reward of *calliditas*. Experience – being worn in the ways of the world – and the impermeability of the hide are both products of the master's anger.

The slave's license

If the slave is what the free person is not, then not only is he a lower form of being but he also has a license to indulge those impulses that the free must subject to rigorous control. What Lott (1995) says about blackface entertainment, citing Žižek's theories on the theft of pleasure, has much to tell us about the mechanisms of Plautine comedy. "Because one is

[24] For *calliditas* as a quality of the slave, see *Amphitryon* 268 and also Ulpian, *Digest* 474.1.pr.1.
[25] Compare *Bacchides* 268–71, where the slave Chrysalus says his master can go to hell (*vapulet*, literally "be beaten") since there's no punishment that he hasn't already experienced.

ambivalent about and represses one's own pleasure, one imagines the Other to have stolen it away, and 'fantasies about the Other's special, excessive enjoyment' allow that pleasure to return. Whites get satisfaction in supposing the 'racial' Other enjoys in ways unavailable to them – through exotic food, strange and noisy music, outlandish bodily exhibitions, or unremitting sexual appetite. And at the same time, because the Other personifies their inner divisions, hatred of their own excess of enjoyment necessitates hatred of the Other. Ascribing this excess to the 'degraded' blackface Other and indulging it – by imagining, incorporating, or impersonating the Other – workingmen confronting the demand to be 'respectable' might at once take their pleasure and disavow it" (148).

The prologue to Plautus' *Poenulus* provides a striking illustration of the ambivalence described by Lott. As the play is about to start, the prologue addresses various groups that must remember their place if the play is to be enjoyed by its proper audience. The noisy gathering must now be silent, both those who wisely have already eaten and those who have come unbreakfasted and must satisfy themselves with plays (*fabulae*, 8). Slaves must let the free sit and not usurp their place unless they can pay for their freedom. If they can't, let them go home and await their masters' return, or else be marked (*varientur*, 26) by the lictors' rods here and by their masters' lash at home. Nurses should take care of their little charges at home so that they don't go thirsty themselves and the hungry children bleat like goats. Matrons should watch silently and laugh silently so as not to be burdens to their husbands both here and at home. But while the show is on, attendant slaves (*pedisequi*, 41) should seize the opportunity to make an assault on the cook-shop (*popina*, 41), now that the cakes are hot. Suddenly, the clearing of space for the free adult male has been diverted by another agenda, the licensing of those excluded from the spectacle to give uninhibited rein to their appetites and steal a march on the orderly rows of seated spectators, some of whom must now be satisfied with drama rather than food. Since these stories themselves feature slaves unburdened by the self-control the free must impose on their own unruly appetites, this imagining of slaves run loose on the city and its delights has a clear connection to the pleasure the play will offer its spectators.[26] In this prologue, the other place where slaves take liber-

---

[26] For a very different relation between slaves in the audience and slaves on the stage, see Thalmann (1997), 119.

ties is not only the imaginary Greece of the comedy itself but the Rome that has been vacated by its free citizens, creating a space where what the free repress is given rein. The *Poenulus* prologue neatly encapsulates the combination of discipline and license to which the Plautine slave is subjected, and in the slave who raids the cook-shop it gives us the flip-side of Horace's Davus: instead of the slave who speaks for, and as, the conscience of his master, we have the slave who indulges the appetites the master must control.

But as we will see in more detail in chapter 4, it is not always the slave who is the main exponent of comic mischief. In some cases the father himself takes over the roles of both lover and slave, concocting a scheme to satisfy his unruly desires, usually in competition with his son (e.g. *Asinaria*, *Casina*). As with Shakespeare's Falstaff and Hoffmansthal's Baron Ochs, his enterprise is doomed to failure, and in the final scene he is dragged away from his pleasures by his wife, trembling, like a slave, with the fear of a beating (*Asinaria*, 936). In the *Casina*, as we shall see, the *senex* very clearly adopts the language and manner of the slave to appeal for mercy. But at the end of the *Asinaria* the appeal is made by the epilogue, who excuses Demaenetus inasmuch as he has done nothing that any red-blooded member of the audience would not also have done. He then concludes the play with the words: "Now if you want to plead for this *senex* to be let off a beating, we think you'll be successful if you applaud loudly" (946–7).[27] In Rome, the epitome of letting someone "get away with it" is letting the slave off a beating, and the actor playing the *senex* in *Asinaria* might in fact have been a slave; whatever his status, the *infamia* (disgrace) that the law attached to him as actor made him subject to beating and so assimilated him to a slave.[28] So the *senex* who finds himself in the role of a slave is in reality a slave (or "slave") playing the role of the *senex*. What results is a complicated moment in which the willingness, even desire, of the audience to sympathize transgressively with the unruly and indecorous appetites of the *senex amator* is overlaid with the proper exercise of judgment by the free over the performance of a slave.

[27] Slater (1985), 67–9. Compare *Cistellaria* 785.
[28] *Amphitruo*, 26–31: 'Jupiter' fears whipping, because he's only a slave (compare Seneca, *Ep*.80, 7–8). Jory (1966) takes a sceptical look at some of the evidence for the slave status of actors. On actors as *infames*, see Edwards (1997).

Plautus' reminder of the player's servility is an example of the meta-theater that pervades his work and is more often than not practiced by the slave characters. The slave, as a figure who is marginal to the social world of the other free characters, is in a position to move between the world of the dramatic fiction and that of the audience. Since he is privy to all the goings-on in the household he is also best placed to keep the audience apprised of plot developments.[29] But, most importantly, it is the clever slave who is responsible for the "plot" – both the scheme *in* the play and the dramatic shape *of* the play – so he can justly be represented as a playwright himself.[30] This is the case with the most virtuosic of Plautus' scheming slaves, the Pseudolus of the play that bears his name, who makes an elaborate comparison of his scheming to the plotting of a playwright (401–5).

Pseudolus' plot resembles a game, or a play. He announces to his master, Simo, that he intends to cheat him out of the money needed to free his son's beloved, now in the hands of an unscrupulous pimp, and challenges Simo to be on his guard (511 and 517). Simo responds by affirming his mastery – Pseudolus will never pull this off, just let him try. And so the master has been provoked into a game that has put his mastery at stake, a game no master would actually have countenanced. Simo's friend, Callipho, suggests that one motive for allowing the slave to attempt his stunt is the motive of the playgoer: "I want to watch your show, Pseudolus," he says, (*lubidost ludos tuos spectare, Pseudole*, 552), taking the role of the spectator seduced by aesthetic suspense into iden-tifying with the slave against his own social position.[31] In the process, Callipho finds himself behaving like the *erro*, the dilatory slave who is sidetracked from his assignment by a typically slavish tendency to gawk.[32] Pseudolus forbids Callipho to commit himself to any other business for the day (549). When the latter replies that he had planned to go to the country, Pseudolus peremptorily orders him to put off his plans (*at nunc disturba quas statuisti machinas*, 550) and Callipho agrees, telling Pseudolus to "proclaim" his "games"(*indice ludos nunciam*, 546). The slave has become a magistrate in a reversal of status reflecting typically

---

[29] On metatheatricality and the servant in European comedy, see Robbins (1986), 54ff.

[30] Slater (1985), 12–13 and passim. Menander's Daos in the *Aspis* (329–30) provides a Greek precedent.

[31] Sharrock (1996), in a metaliterary reading of the play, has some good remarks on Callipho and the audience (164–5).   [32] Bradley (1990), 144 on the *erro*.

Roman anxieties that the (slavish) entertainer may exercise a sway over the entertained.[33]

Earlier, confessing that he has no plan for making good on the promise he has made to his young master to swindle Simo out of the necessary money, Pseudolus compares himself to a playwright:

> sed quasi poeta, tabulas quom cepit sibi,
> quaerit quod nusquam gentiumst, reperit tamen,
> facit illud veri simile quod mendacium est,
> nunc ego poeta fiam: viginti minas,
> quae nusquam sunt gentium, inveniam tamen.   (401–5)

> But just as a poet, when he takes up his tablets,
> searches for what is nowhere, but still finds it,
> making what is a lie seem like truth,
> now I will become a poet: I'll find
> the twenty minae which are nowhere.

The predicament of the slave injects drama into the creation of drama itself, for on this analogy the playwright doesn't just invent a plausible story, he turns a lie into reality, and does so under considerable pressure. This pressure to perform, which Pseudolus has himself created, becomes a figure for the expectant audience's relation to the plot as it develops before their eyes.

After the scene in which the terms of the bet between Simo and Pseudolus have been set, Pseudolus addresses the audience as follows:

> suspicio est mi nunc vos suspicarier
> me idcirco haec tanta facinora promittere,
> qui vos oblectem, hanc fabulam dum transigam,
> neque sim facturus quod facturum dixeram.
> non demutabo. atque etiam certum, quod sciam,
> quo id sim facturus pacto nihil etiam scio,
> nisi quia futurumst. nam qui in scaenam provenit,
> novo modo novom aliquid inventum adferre addecet;
> si id facere nequeat, det locum illi qui queat.   (562–70)

> I suspect that you suspect
> I'm promising all these feats

---

[33] Fitzgerald (1995), 56–8.

Just to amuse you while I act out this play,
And that I won't do what I have said I would do.
I won't renege. Though, as far as I know,
I don't know how I'm going to do it, only that I will.
For anyone who comes on stage
must bring on some new invention in some new style;
if he can't do that, let him give way to someone who can.

The relationship between slave and masters on the stage is here applied to that between playwright and audience, which gives urgency to the demand that the playwright (through the actor) bring on something new. But the comparison is not entirely a figure of speech, as the references to the servile status of actors at the end of *Asinaria* and *Cistellaria* indicate: actors who didn't deliver might be beaten. Playwrights too might be of servile or freedman status.[34] But if entertaining is a slavish occupation, catering to the pleasures of others, it is one in which the entertained are in the ambiguous position of both passing judgment and suspending their authority in the throes of aesthetic fascination.

In his wonder at Pseudolus' boldness, Callipho acclaims him as a *graphicus* if he can deliver on his bet. The Greek loan-word, meaning "worthy to be drawn", figures Pseudolus both as a precious possession plundered from Greece and an example of Greek mastery.[35] Pseudolus takes up the figure a few lines later when he protests, in response to Simo's suspicion that he is in league with the pimp:

aut si de istac re umquam inter nos convenimus
quasi in libro quom scribuntur calamo litterae,
stilis me totum usque ulmeis conscribito.   (544–5)

Or if we have come to an agreement between ourselves in this affair
scribble all over me with elm rods
just as letters are written in a book with a reed.

[34] Livius Andronicus, Caecilius Statius and Terence were all freedmen, as was the mime writer Publilius Syrus.

[35] Notice that Pseudolus breaks into Greek when he is being cross-questioned by Simo, 483ff. Fraenkel (1960) argues that Plautus' use of the Greek words *basilice* and *graphicus*, usually applied to slaves, is not derived from Greek comic models (183–6). Plautus has gone out of his way to associate the heroic slave with "Greekness."

Having earlier compared himself to a playwright, tablets in hand, ponder-ing a new device, Pseudolus now reassures his audience as to who has the ultimate power to write the script. If he is a *graphicus* to be admired, he is also the surface on which the free can write at will. The pen is in the other hand.[36] Though the pun associating literacy with punishment goes back to Aristophanes (πολυγράμματος, *Frag.* 64), it acquires a new resonance in its Roman context, where educated Greek slaves were much in demand, but awakened mixed emotions in their less cultured Roman owners.[37]

In view of Pseudolus' previous comparison of himself to a playwright there is clearly a metatheatrical dimension to this scene. But the scene not only uses the relation between slave and master to dramatize the relation between playwright/actor and audience; it also allows us to glimpse the complex of motives that might draw a master into allowing a slave to dictate the rules of engagement. Not that such a challenge as Pseudolus' could ever have been made by a slave or accepted by a master, but the ludicrousness of this scene results from magnifying something plausibly real: the master's need for, and enjoyment of, a certain drama within the master/slave relationship. Simo accepts, and relishes, the opportunity to *prove* his mastery, just as Xanthos issues challenges to Aesop. The impli-cation of Callipho's "*graphicus*," as of Pseudolus' "graphic" image of beating, is that there may be a conflict between the master's need to exer-cise his mastery and his desire to admire his property, a conflict that could be manipulated, on some level, by a clever slave, especially one prized for his very cleverness.

Love and shaving

A delicate, and always revocable, suspension of master-slave relations was required for some roles that the slave might be called upon to play, most obviously the role of beloved, where the master might want to imagine a degree of reciprocity between him and the *delicatus*.[38] Martial's Telesphorus, a young boy who served as a cupbearer (cf. 11.26), is repre-sented as neither entirely free to dispose of his body nor entirely at the dis-posal of his master. Lying with him, Martial asks (11.26) for kisses wet with

---

[36] Compare the pun on *litteratus* at *Casina* 401.

[37] For instance Plutarch, *Cato* 20.4.

[38] Kolendo (1981) on sex and slaves; Garrido-Hory (1981), chapter 6 on Martial, sex and slaves.

the Falernian he has just served his master; but if Telesphorus should allow him "the true joys of Venus" (*Veneris . . . gaudia vera*) he'll be as happy as Jove with his Ganymede. The erotic game requires the slave to be neither too willing nor too grudging. In 11.58 Telesphorus has been pushing his luck:

> Cum me velle vides tentumque, Telesphore, sentis,
> > magna rogas – puta me velle negare; licet? –
> et nisi iuratus dixi 'dabo,' subtrahis illas,
> > permittunt in me quae tibi multa, natis.
> quid si me tonsor, cum stricta novacula supra est,
> > tunc libertatem divitiasque roget?
> promittam; neque enim rogat illo tempore tonsor,
> > latro rogat; res est imperiosa timor:
> sed fuerit curva cum tuta novacula theca,
> > frangam tonsori crura manusque simul.
> at tibi nil faciam, sed lota mentula lana
> > λαικάζειν cupidae dicet avarititiae.

> When you see that I want it, Telesphorus, and that I'm stiff
> > you make demands – suppose I want to deny you; could I?
> and until I've promised and said "I'll give" you deny me
> > those buttocks which give you power over me.
> Imagine my barber, with drawn razor flashing,
> > should then demand freedom and riches –
> I would promise: for it's not a barber who's asking
> > but a thief; fear is an imperious emotion.
> But once the blade was safely in the curved sheath,
> > I would break the barber's legs and his hands too.
> You I won't punish, but once it's been wiped off
> > my prick will tell your greed to go to hell.

The brutality envisaged for the hypothetical barber reminds Telesphorus of his true position, and at the same time of the immunity he enjoys as *delicatus*, an immunity that can always be revoked. What is most remarkable about the comparison, though, is the way that the phallus passes from Martial (*tentum . . . sentis*) to the slave as barber (*stricta novacula*) and back again (*lota mentula lana*). The barber's razor returned safely to its sheath metamorphoses into Martial's wiped penis to compensate for the fact that the boy's *with*drawing of his buttocks became the equivalent of the barber's drawn razor, itself a figure for the master's own erect penis (*tentum*) turned against him (*permittunt in me*). Martial's two instances of the vulnerable master mutually ameliorate each other: the humiliating situation of being at the mercy of the slave barber is assuaged by the master's penetration of the *delicatus*, while the boy's sway over his master is compensated by the punishment envisaged for the barber who takes advantage of his temporary position. Martial's fantasy of the barber asking for freedom and riches may be as unlikely as the boy's sexual manipulation is plausible, but the collocation is revealing, for it places this particular relation between master and *delicatus* in a more general context. If the slave is to serve his master properly, the master must sometimes put his person at the slave's disposal.

One can well believe that the experience of being shaved by a slave might give rise to horrible imaginings in the master. After all, here is the slave he had beaten applying a (reasonably) sharp blade to his throat! Cicero tells us of a master who had his hair singed off with a glowing coal, for fear of the barber's razor (*De Officiis*, 2.25). In another poem of Martial (11.84) his incompetent barber covers his master's face with cuts, which the poet refers to as *stigmata*, the tattoos that marked the face of a runaway slave.[39] Revenge indeed! According to Robbins, the shaving of the master takes on revolutionary connotations in the modern European novel, figuring sometimes the guillotine and at other times sexual humiliation or castration.[40] In Martial's poem, the castration anxiety raised by the proximity of razor and penis may have to do with subtler fears than those of revolution. If, as Aristotle puts it, the slave is a living part of the master's body, but detached from him, then the master is indeed potentially castrated. It is because the slave performs the work of the master's limbs in their stead that he can be said to be a part of the master's body. When ancient writers expressed concern that the master might become dependent on the slave, they sometimes correlated dependence with the loss of limbs or bodily functions on the part of the master. In a famous anecdote the sight of a man having his shoe tied by a slave caused Diogenes to remark "You have not attained to full felicity, unless he wipes your nose as well; and that will come, when you have lost the use of your hands" (Diogenes Laertius 6.45.13). Pliny (*N.H.*29.19) makes a similar point: "We walk with another's feet, read with

---

[39] Compare the haircutting metaphor at *Captivi* 266–70. On tattooing, see Jones (1987).   [40] Robbins (1993), 139–44.

another's eyes, greet with another's memory, live with alien performance. Natural things have lost their value, and with them the substance of life is lost." When the master's erect penis metamorphoses into the barber's naked blade (and back) Martial's poem stumbles into areas that have more to do with being served than with sex.

The violence in Martial's little vignette of the barber, breaking out against the slave who has presumed too much on his license, reminds the boy of the license his master has over him. As a being without rights or honor, the slave can be treated and exploited like an animal or a thing, but as a human the slave has more to offer if given a degree of autonomy. The uncertainties that follow from this instability only increase the violence that always hovers over the relation between master and slave, and they nurture a distinctly schizophrenic atmosphere. Let me end this chapter with a striking example of this schizophrenia in Ausonius' aubade to the sleeping Parmeno ("Trusty"). Ausonius' *Ephemeris* is an account of his daily routine, perhaps inspired by school exercises used to teach Latin and Greek; both Ausonius' poems and the exercises prominently feature orders given to a slave at every juncture of the day.[41] *Ephemeris* opens with a poem addressed to his slave, which begins with affectionate teasing of the snoring Parmeno: the dormice sleep all winter long, but they ration their food; Parmeno by contrast is sleeping off the effects of too much food and drink. The banter then veers suddenly and seamlessly, via an allusion to Horace,[42] into another mode, threatening Parmeno with beating, even death: *surge, nugator, lacerande virgis,/ surge, ne longus tibi somnus, unde/ non times, detur* (17–19). The final stanza puts this alternation of attitude in a neat generic context:

> fors et haec somnum tibi cantilena
> Sapphico suadet modulata versu;
> Lesbiae depelle modum quietis,
>   acer iambe.

> Perhaps this ditty in the Sapphic mode
> is swaying you to sleep;
> repel the drowsy Lesbian rhythm,
>   bitter iambic.

---

[41] Dionisotti (1982).   [42] Horace C.3.11.38–9.

3

Slaves between the free

A great deal of business, in every sense of the word, was conducted between the free through slave intermediaries, constantly available as buffers, proxies, substitutes, fall-guys, and messengers.[1] Slaves provided the free with leeway in their relations with each other, and they also enabled a set of relations shadowing those with their peers, both a convenience and a source of friction. The present chapter concerns these triangular relations between slaves and free.

Nowhere did slavery affect relations between the free more acutely than in the Roman family. The very words *domus* and *familia* had a capacious semantic range, including (sometimes, but not always) both slaves and family in a single unit. Seneca, for instance, (*De Ira* 3.35.1) lists slaves, freedmen and clients, together with wife, as part of the *domus*. It is not until modern times that such usages fade to isolate starkly the nuclear family as an affective and domestic unit.[2] Within the Roman house, slave nurses and *paedagogi* would stand in for parents in some areas of the care and education of the children and, conversely, one or more of the slave *familia* might actually be children of the *paterfamilias*, and a slave or freedwoman his *concubina*.[3] The legalities of the situation could get complicated, and they offered rich opportunities for the exercise of legal and rhetorical ingenuity.[4] Martial (6.39) displays his literary wit on a wildly paradoxical menage in which it is the *matrona*, not the *paterfamilias*, who is confusing the situation: Cinna has been made a father seven times by

---

[1] Business: Thebert (1993), 156–8.
[2] Williams (1983), 131–4; Stone (1977), 24–6; Fairchild (1984),137–40 and 152–3.
[3] Bradley (1991) and Joshel (1986) on nurses; Treggiari (1981) on *concubinae*.
[4] A good example in Wallace-Hadrill (1994), 176–8.

his wife Marulla, but not a father of children/freeborn (*non liberorum*),[5] for his wife has been doing the rounds of the slaves. Her thoroughness leads to the miraculous circumstance of Cinna's becoming a father by his own *concubinus* (13), and this in turn makes new liaisons possible: "Go ahead and screw (*percide*) your son," says Martial "it's not a sin" (14). In legal terms, the child born to a free woman was free, and if she was married that child was presumed to be the husband's offspring, but there was a strong taboo against sex between a free woman and a slave, in contrast to the permissive attitude to sex between a free man and a slave.[6] In another poem on sex between free and slave (1.84), Martial puns on *paterfamilias* to bear down on the ambiguity of the word *familia*: Quirinalis wants to have children but does not want to marry, so he fucks his maids and fills the fields with homeborn slaves that are knights, or vice versa (*equitibus vernis*, 4). "You could certainly call him a father of the *familia*" (*pater familiae verus est Quirinalis*, 5). The pun is an ironic confirmation of the success of Quirinalis' project, mocking him with a disgraceful title. But the fact that this title is almost indistinguishable from the most august of Roman appellations directs some of the irony against the unstable category of the *familia*. With these puns on *liberi* and *paterfamilias* Martial conjures up a world that is both parallel and internal to the world of the free.

Quirinalis, as his name reminds us, is not doing his duty by the *respublica*, which has a legitimate stake in the marriage and fatherhood of Roman citizens.[7] It was one of the conveniences of slaves that they allowed the master to isolate certain aspects of human relationships from the burdensome ramifications of their social embedding. Roman law, for instance, recognized an exclusive relation with a slave (concubinage) as an alternative to marriage. Young men like St Augustine found this a convenient way of satisfying their physical and emotional needs before a traditionally late marriage.[8] For a widower, to take a *concubina* rather than a second wife allowed him to avoid introducing a stepmother into the family and so confusing existing arrangements for distribution of property.[9] Concubinage was regarded as a perfectly honorable estate for both

---

[5] On the semantic relation between *liber* and *liberi*, see Benveniste (1936).

[6] Watson (1987), 10–11.

[7] Treggiari (1991), 8–9. The phrase "*liberorum quaerendorum gratia*" (for the purpose of producing children) seems to have been part of the Roman marriage ceremony.

[8] Brown (1967), 62–3.   [9] Saller (1987) 74–6.

partners; other less formal sexual relations between masters and their slaves (sometimes loosely called *concubinae/i* as well) might awaken comment, as in the case of Martial's Quirinalis. Since Quirinalis is bypassing the demands of society and the state to create a legitimate family, society strikes back with mockery. A similar kind of objection lies behind three poems in which Martial castigates people who have sold their fields to buy slave boys (9.21; 12.16; 12.33). Double entendres are deployed to pit the traditional Roman values of agriculture against the "Greek" luxuries of pederasty (*arat/amat* in 9.21.4), the fruitful against the barren. For instance, Labienus (12.33), who has sold his estates for boys, is left now only with a fig-orchard (*ficetum*, with a pun on *ficus* = hemorrhoid).

But relationships that sidestepped the awkward ramifications and responsibilities pertaining among the free could also be presented in a positive light, as purely affective. A good freedman, says a character in Publilius Syrus (450), is a son "*sine natura*," and this absence of nature need not be seen as a lack. Statius, in one of several poems on the death of a patron's *delicatus,* makes the case for the importance of elective as well as natural affinities:

> non omnia sanguis
> proximus aut serie generis demissa propago
> alligat; interius nova saepe adscitaque serpunt
> pignora conexis. natos genuisse necesse est,
> elegisse iuvat.   (*Silvae* 2.1.84–8)

> Closeness of blood
> or the descent of the family tree are not the only
> ties; newly adopted children often insinuate themselves
> more intimately. Bringing children to birth is a necessity,
> choosing them a pleasure.[10]

Statius can't entirely dispense with the authority of the ties of nature, though, and he first establishes that this *delicatus* was a *verna*, born and bred in the house, not a bought slave (*empticius*) who had seduced his master with prepared words (72–8).

---

[10] On this poem, see Van Dam (1984), especially 69–73 on *delicatus* and 68 on *puer* (son/slave).

In his potted autobiography, Petronius' Trimalchio tells us that he had been a *puer delicatus*, servicing both master and mistress (whom he "thumped": *ut ego sic solebam ipsumam meam debattuere*, 69!). Eventually he inherited his master's fortune and now he himself has a *delicatus* whom he calls, appropriately, Croesus (64). His guest, Habinnas, is accompanied by a *delicatus* whom he indulges outrageously, much to the disgust of his wife and the guests (68–69). Habinnas is proud of his boy. His only drawbacks are that he is circumcised and he snores; as for the fact that he is squint-eyed, isn't that how Venus looks? The freedman's dubious taste in boys is meant to raise a laugh, but he is also claiming authenticity for his relationship by preferring good character to physical beauty. One anonymous author of an epitaph goes so far as to acknowledge that his *delicatus* was not even good-looking: Venus' charms were less apparent in his face than in his heart (*te sortita Paphon pulchro minus ore notabat / diva, set in toto corde plicata inerat*).[11] The epitaph goes on to praise the deceased for his *simplicitas facilis*; Courtney translates "obliging frankness," which catches nicely the paradoxical combination of qualities that are appropriate to, and treasured in, an inferior. Clearly one of the factors that promoted close emotional ties between masters and slaves was the intensely competitive relation between coevals in Roman society. Many of the famous friendships in the Roman world were between people separated by age, status or career. Atticus, for instance, who did not choose to pursue office, could be no rival to Cicero and hence became a treasured confidant and intimate; Caelius was many years his junior and the indispensable Tiro a slave.[12]

Depending on how one chose to look at it, the relationship between master and *delicatus* might appear selfish, irresponsible and self-indulgent, or truly authentic, altruistic and deeply felt. Speaking of the death of his slave girl Erotion, not yet six years old (5.37, cf. 5.34), Martial protests against a friend who disapproves of his grief,

> et esse tristem me meus vetat Paetus.
> pectusque pulsans pariter et comam vellens:
> "deflere non te vernulae pudet mortem?
> ego coniugem" inquit "extuli et tamen vivo,
> notam, superbam, nobilem, locupletem."

---

[11] *CIL* 3.686, 7–8. Text, translation and commentary in Courtney (1995), 174–5 and 384–6.   [12] Habinek (1990).

quid esse nostro fortius potest Paeto?
ducentiens accepit et tamen vivit.   (18–24)

And my friend Paetus says I shouldn't grieve.
He strikes his breast and tears his hair as well:
"Aren't you ashamed to mourn the death of a houseborn slave?
I've buried my wife" he says "and yet I live,
although she was noted, proud, noble and rich."
What could be braver than my friend Paetus?
He inherited twenty million and yet he lives.

Paetus' adjectives allude to the broader issues that surround a Roman marriage, from which Martial selects the last, money, for his coup de grace. Although Erotion was her master's property, the relationship between them, as Martial would have it, was untainted by the kind of considerations that made Roman marriage more (or less) than an affective bond.

Slaves and guests

Standing at the interface between private and public, slaves provided a window onto the private affairs of the family. Martial makes it clear that the disposition and treatment of slaves in the household was subject to the judgment, and sometimes the intervention, of guests. He accuses Cinna of gluttony because his cook is a boy surpassing his cup-bearers in beauty (12.64), and is himself criticized, by the significantly named Rusticus, for beating his cook after a disappointing meal (above, chapter 2). Elsewhere, Martial finds that the disposition of slaves betrays dirty little secrets of the master's and mistress's relationship: "Linus, your wife has indicated what she suspects of you by giving you a eunuch doorman" (2.54); "Magulla, you share a bed and a concubine (*exoletus*) with your husband, why not a waiter? There's a reason: you fear the wine-flask [i.e. poison]" (12.91).[13]

Since the master's treatment of his slaves was part of his public image, the slave might acquire some leverage on his master through the guests; not only that, but the etiquette of hospitality included deference to a guest who urged leniency for a slave threatened with punishment.[14] Twice

---

[13] For Martial on slaves, see Garrido-Hory (1981).
[14] A commonly represented episode of Roman life, Veyne (1987), 65.

during Trimalchio's banquet in the *Satyricon* of Petronius a slave falls at the feet of the guests and begs to be let off a punishment he has incurred (30; 54).[15] In the first case, the guests beg the steward to exercise mercy and he "makes a present" of the slave, who expresses his gratitude with the revealing proverb "the master's wine is the slave's thanks" (31). In the second episode, the always unpredictable Trimalchio anticipates his guests by finding a perverse reason to forgive the slave his transgression.[16] The most famous example of a guest's intervention in the punishment of a slave is the story of the rich knight Vedius Pollio, who was entertaining Augustus when one of his slaves broke an expensive crystal bowl (Seneca *De Ira* 3.40.2 and Dio Cassius 54.23.1ff.). When Vedius ordered the slave to be thrown into his fish-pond as live bait for the lampreys, the slave threw himself at the emperor's feet and begged to be allowed to die in some other way. Augustus not only pardoned the boy, but, so appalled was he at his host's cruelty, he had all of Vedius' crystal smashed and the fish-pond filled in.

Deferring to a female guest in the matter of a slave might be a way for the master to advance his suit. Ovid advises the lover to let his mistress think she has obtained freedom for a slave to whom he has already promised it, and similarly with remitting a punishment (*Ars Amatoria* 2. 287). In Chariton's *Callirhoe*, Dionysius endears himself to his beautiful slave Callirhoe by giving the impression that she has secured a pardon for the bailiff Phocas (2.7).[17]

Paedagogus and whipping-boy

Punishment itself might introduce triangular relations between slaves and free, especially since not all free people were immune to punishment and the administering of punishment was usually the work of slaves.[18] I will consider the overlap in status (and nomenclature) between child and slave in chapter 4, but for the moment we should remember that it was predominantly slaves who disciplined the children of their masters,

---

[15] Compare the episode of the busybody in the *Life of Aesop* (57–9).

[16] Dumont (1987), 383 cites Donatus, who quotes typical phrases of intercessors (Donatus *ad* Ter. *Ph.*, 140–3).

[17] Pliny (*Ep.*1.4) shows that guests might be used to keep slaves on their toes, an interesting reversal of what I have been discussing. I owe this reference to Kathleen McCarthy.   [18] Aulus Gellius 103.18–19 (on *lorarii*).

standing, in this case, *in loco parentis*. Slave *paedagogi* were probably the most immediate voices of authority for young members of the Roman elite and they were empowered to beat their free charges.[19] The breadth of the *paedagogus'* field of influence is conveyed by a poem of Martial (11.39) in which, adopting the persona of a young man who has recently attained his majority, he complains to the slave Charidemus who looked after him from the cradle that he still regards his erstwhile charge as a boy. Charidemus numbers his cups at dinner, disapproves of his extravagant dress and his amours ("Your father never would have done that") and scarcely restrains himself from reaching for the cane. Pistoclerus in Plautus' *Bacchides* makes a similar point against his *paedagogus* Lydus, who disapproves of his amour (*Bacch*.129). When Pistoclerus' father takes the side of his son, Lydus reminds us of the ironies of the slave-tutor's position: how can he exert discipline if he himself is beaten? (447–8). Such things must have happened.

The reverse of the *paedagogus*, who spares the father the job of disciplining his son, would be the whipping-boy, the slave who is punished in the place of the free. An anecdote about the scholar Ammonius recorded by Plutarch (*Moralia* 70E) provides an interesting example. Feeling that his students had been insufficiently frugal with their lunch, Ammonius had a slave beaten during the afternoon lecture to provide them with a warning on the necessity of self-control ("That boy can't lunch without his wine"). The students were learning something about their own status, subordinate and yet free, but the most striking aspect of this story is the way that messages pass between the free through the slave: the teacher's dissatisfaction with the students is read through his treatment of the slave. Other teachers were more direct.[20]

Fall guys and alibis

Normal relations between the free were constantly mediated by slaves. It was the slaves (and, in the case of the emperor, freedmen) who controlled access to the master and directed the flow of people in the house.[21] Household slaves were responsible for preventing theft (Juvenal 5.40–1).

[19] [Cicero] *Ad Her*.4.10.14. On *paedagogi*, see Bradley (1991), 37–74.
[20] Most famously, Horace's teacher (*plagosus*) Orbilius (*Ep.* 2.1.70).
[21] Wallace-Hadrill (1994), 39.

Doubtless it was convenient for the master to delegate unpleasant and embarrassing communications to his slave, and if this was so it was partly because the slave was not regarded as simply an extension of the master's will. Blaming the slave was a convenient way of avoiding embarrassment. When Martial takes an acquaintance to task for not inviting him to his birthday party he imagines the other responding with the ancient equivalent of blaming the mail: the slave charged with the invitations will be beaten (7.86, *vapulet vocator*). On another occasion, a hostess called Naevia is pilloried for her meanness (3.13): she spares the fish, fowl and boar, but beats the cook as though he has brought the meat to the table raw.

In public, any free person of substance was cushioned and bolstered by one or more accompanying slaves, who cleared a passage through crowds, often jostling free men in the process. For a free person to be elbowed by someone else's slave might be less insulting than to suffer the same thing at the hand of a peer; the same logic led the Athenians to employ Scythian archers to arrest and detain other free citizens. Pliny (*Ep*.3.14) tells how Larcius Macedo was struck by a knight when Macedo's slave touched the knight in the process of making way for his master in the Baths. Pliny regards it as an omen of Macedo's subsequent murder by his own slaves that the knight struck him and not the slave. This breakdown of the usually reliable servile cushion between the free is for Pliny a premonition of the catastrophic collapse of the barrier between master and slave when Macedo's slaves turn on him and kill him.

So the slave-intermediary, as a semi-distinct being, allowed some room for play in the relations between masters – one could strike the slave, not the master.[22] And yet, at the same time, the slave represented the master, which led to the awkward consequence that some slaves had to be treated with the respect appropriate to a superior. The status of another's trusted slaves was always complicated by the fact that they were delegates of a peer or superior, and controlled access to their masters. This meant that there was an asymmetry between one's own slaves, who were clearly one's subordinates, and those of a peer or superior, who bore some of the status of their master. Seneca milks the paradoxes of this asymmetry when castigating a harsh master "for whom the kiss of another's slave is a favor ... at the same time you despise the slave and cultivate him, imper-

---

[22] See Joshel (1992), 76 on Juvenal 5.24–79.

ious and uncontrolled at home, humble abroad and as much despised as despising" (*De Beneficiis* 3.28.5).[23]

Go-betweens: Ovid, *Amores* 1.11 and 12.

Almost any scene between two people at Rome was attended by one or more slaves. Even the most intimate and secret relationships could not dispense with a messenger, go-between or attendant. Love affairs, licit or illicit, inevitably involved slaves, and not only as facilitators. Jealous husbands relied on slaves to chaperone their wives and keep them out of harm's way: Ovid (*Amores* 2.2–3) tries to persuade the eunuch Bagoas delegated to watch over his master's wife that his best interests lie in helping rather than hindering his mistress's affair. The presence of slaves is one of the most likely intrusions on privacy, and Martial remarks on the luxury of not having slaves overhearing you when you travel (12.24), and on the fact that a deaf mule-driver fetches a high price (11.38).[24] Slaves, of course, were in a position to betray the master's or mistress's weaknesses to other free people, and the fear of this possibility might provoke cruelty: "Ponticus, why do you crucify your slave with his tongue cut out? Don't you know that people are gossiping about what he keeps silent?" (Martial, 2.82) A more enlightened way to deal with the problem is recommended by Seneca, who urges Lucilius to let his slaves talk freely in his presence so that they remain silent under torture (*Ep*.47.4). Perhaps the fact that slaves could only give evidence in court under torture served, among other things, to mark as extreme the conditions under which a slave might reveal the secrets of his owners to their peers. Otherwise, nobody was safe.

Slave attendants might be the invisible tracks that enabled relations between the free to run smoothly or they might come into focus as beings with a presence and humanity that made them actors in their own right. Most often, no doubt, they shifted in and out of the focus of the free. For many purposes, the intermediary slave might be required to exercise an initiative, or at the very least a tact, that could not be anticipated in the master's or mistress's orders, an intiative that presupposed a more than servile spirit and understanding. But how much initiative was too much? As we have seen, the *Life of Aesop* capitalizes on this problem to great comic effect. Two pairs of poems from Ovid's *Amores* (1.11 and 12, 2.7

---

[23] Cf. Seneca, *Ep* 47.14.   [24] Compare Apuleius, *Golden Ass* 2.15.

and 8) play with the ambiguity of the slave-intermediary's status with considerable subtlety, as John Henderson has shown, among other things, in two splendid articles (1991 and 1992). Many of the points I will be making can be found somewhere in his exhaustive treatment, though my framework is rather different.

Amores 1.11 and 12 feature the maid Nape, a hairdresser, who is to deliver a message to Corinna.[25] In the first poem Nape, who has in the past been a faithful adjutant to Ovid in his pursuit of Corinna, is charged with delivering the tablets with his message. She is to choose an opportune moment, read Corinna's reactions and urge her to respond. But the end of the poem veers away from Nape, who has been flattered and briefed throughout and concludes :

> non ego victrices lauro redimire tabellas
> > nec Veneris media ponere in aede morer;
> subscribam VENERI FIDAS SIBI NASO MINISTRAS
> > DEDICAT. AT NUPER VILE FUISTIS ACER.

> I would not hesitate to wreathe with laurel the victorious tablets
> > nor to set them up in Venus' own house;
> I will inscribe "Naso dedicates to Venus his faithful servants
> > but just recently you were cheap maple."

The poem that had begun with Nape, the maid who is too *docta* to be counted among the servants (2), ends with a promise of promotion for the *tablets*, "faithful servants"! Nape is praised as an appropriate messenger because she is more than a slave, but it is the tablets that will become more than mere wood as a reward for carrying Ovid's message faithfully. Once the task has been successfully performed, the slave returns to the status of an instrument. As we will see, there is a constant slippage in this poem between tablets and maid, the two media of Ovid's message, and this slippage betrays the essential ambiguity of the slave as mediator. Is she the faithful parrot or the skilful ambassador?

In the following poem, Ovid laments the return of the tablets with Corinna's refusal. At first, Nape is castigated for stumbling on the threshold, a bad omen, but for the rest of the poem the tablets are roundly cursed as wood that came from an ill-omened tree and should never have

---

[25] On these poems, see also the remarks in McCarthy (1998), 182–4.

been turned to human uses. The poem ends by wishing on them an unsightly old age. To compensate for the fact that, at the end of 11, the tablets received the reward that Nape might have expected, at the end of 12 they bear the brunt of accusations that might have been made of her. Nape ("grove" in Greek), enlisted to promote Ovid's love affair, is a living double of the wooden tablets that bear Ovid's message,[26] and in the second poem it is the tablets to whom Ovid has entrusted his love, not Nape:

> his ego commisi nostros insanus amores
> molliaque ad dominam verba ferenda dedi!   (21–2)[27]

> To these I (madman) entrusted my love
> and gave soft words to be brought to my mistress.

After the failure of the letter, the tablets are given an ill-omened history as living wood: the tree from which they came was used for hanging or crucifixion, and gave grim shade to hoarse owls; the hand that shaped them was not pure. This history is precisely not what is required of the inorganic instrument that has been made from the tree. Nape, on the other hand, though only a maid, has a history that makes her apt for Ovid's purposes (*credibile est et te sensisse Cupidinis arcus*, 11.11–12); she is emphatically not inorganic matter (*nec silicum venae nec durum in pectore ferrum*, 11.9). Is the slave more useful to the master if she has a free spirit? Not only is Nape not made of flint or iron, she is also no more simple than is appropriate to her station (*nec tibi simplicitas ordine maior adest*, 10). This lack of *simplicitas* seems to be an advantage in view of her mission, which calls for a certain amount of initiative and knowledge in the ways of the heart. But for the tablets the same does not apply: the tablets (in Greek, δίπτυχα) have been found double, or duplicitous, in more than name (*ergo ego vos rebus duplices pro nomine sensi*, 12.27).[28] Ovid's wordplay reflects an indecision about how the lover's message is best to be conveyed, and specifically about whether the carrier, instrumental or human, is to be a transparent medium or a participating agent.

---

[26] Henderson (1991), 27.   [27] Contrast *tabellas . . . perfer* in *Amores* 1.11.7–8.

[28] As Henderson (1991) points out, the Greek word πτύξ has as one of its meanings "cleft," or "glen," which is related to the meaning of the name Nape (grove).

The lover's mission, and the message to Corinna, was divided between Nape and the tablets; it was itself double in having vocal and written components:

> si quaeret quid agam, spe noctis vivere dices;
> cetera fert blanda cera notata manu.   (11.13–14)

> If she should ask what I'm doing, say I live in hope of a night;
> the rest is told by the wax marked by a caressing hand.

So the written correspondence between Ovid and Corinna needs a supplement, someone to judge the right moment, to read the reading face, to urge an immediate reply. But, in order to carry out this supplementary function, Nape must first interpret Ovid's contradictory orders: "Give them to her when she is free, but make her read them straightaway; tell her to write a long reply, but no, just tell her to write 'Come!'" No wonder Nape is introduced as a hairdresser expert at gathering and styling wayward locks (*colligere incertos et in ordine ponere crines / docta neque ancillas inter habenda Nape*, 11.1–2). To interpret these orders, and to unravel all their ambiguities, requires a Nape who is not herself neatly placed in her *ordo* (rank). She is the supplement needed to control meaning that might otherwise slip, for the written message will not bear its intended sense unless delivered at the right moment and with the right instruction for response, which is a matter for judgment on the spur of the moment. But when the message fails, it is the medium that is accused of being duplicitous, insufficiently transparent and marred by a history of its own. Nape and the tablets are really two aspects of the same problem, and the wordplays that connect them draw attention to the themes of raw material transformed; promotion and demotion along the chain of being; simplicity and duplicity – themes that have a clear relevance to slavery. At the same time, the mediation of the slave, both instrument and adjutant, raises the issue of how and what the message communicates. The slave's ambiguous status as medium of communication between the free makes her the perfect figure to carry anxieties about the adequacy of the written word.[29]

---

[29] McCarthy (1998) 184 reads the failure of both Nape and the tablets as Ovid's way of asserting his independence of these instruments and surrogates (slave and writing).

The go-between as substitute: *Amores* 2.7 and 8

Nape's sophistication, which makes it likely that she herself has felt the arrows of Cupid, allows her to be stand-in, as well as messenger, in Ovid's courtship of Corinna. In another pair of poems, Corinna's sophisticated hairdressing maid becomes a substitute for Corinna herself: *Amores* 2.7 and 8 take up the theme of the *amor servae*, the love of a slave, which balances the *servitium amoris* that the poet-lover himself undergoes.[30] In the *Ars Amatoria,* Ovid discusses the usefulness of the maid as an ally in the lover's suit (1.351–74) and then goes on to debate the merits of raping (*violare,* 375) the maid herself (375–98).[31] His advice is equivocal (it could help or it could hinder; best not to risk it) and ruthless (either don't try or make sure you finish the job). The *Amores* poems are similarly heartless. In the first, Ovid strenuously denies sleeping with Cypassis the maid (a maid, of all things!) and castigates Corinna for her ridiculous suspicions; in the next he accuses Cypassis of giving the game away and demands an assignation on pain of confessing all to her (their) mistress. Much of the second poem replays the scene of the first from a new angle: "How did Corinna find out? My act was perfect (what about the bit when I said only a madman would sleep with a slave?). But you blushed when she looked at you (wasn't my oath a bit of quick thinking?)" The first poem presents an alliance between the two free people, a circle which excludes the slave, and the second a complicity between poet and slave that excludes the mistress. The second poem simultaneously revises the scene of the first poem (two free people were arguing about a slave *in her presence*) and revises this revision (in fact, the slave and the lover were struggling to outwit their mistress).

After a preamble on Corinna's insatiable suspicion, the diptych begins with the accusation:

> nunc temere insimulas credendoque omnia frustra
> > ipsa vetas iram pondus habere tuam:
> aspice, ut auritus miserandae sortis asellus
> > adsiduo domitus verbere lentus eat.

---

[30] On these poems, see Henderson (1991 and 1992) and Yardley (1974), who compares Propertius 3.15 and cites literary parallels for the *amor servae.*

[31] On slave-rape in Ovid, see James (1997).

ecce, novum crimen: sollers ornare Cypassis
        obicitur dominae contemerasse torum.   (*Amores* 2.7.13–18)

Now you rashly accuse me and, by believing everything at random,
        you yourself prevent your anger having any weight.
Look at how the long-eared ass of pitiable fortune
        goes slower under the repeated blows of the whip.
And now, a new accusation: Cypassis, the artful beautician
        is held to have defiled the bed of her mistress.

The long-eared ass is Ovid, the well-endowed lover and *servus amoris*
whose performance may be impaired (*lentus*) by the importunacy of his
mistress. But the long-eared beast of burden is also a figure for the listening slave, present, as we will find out in the next poem, at this lovers'
quarrel in which she is the issue, but referred to only in the third person.[32]
What is a figure of speech with respect to Ovid (worn down not by *verbera*
but by *verba*) may be all too real with reference to his partner, anything
but *lenta* in her lovemaking with Ovid, and perhaps encouraged in this
by her mistress' beatings:

di melius, quam me, si sit peccasse libido,
        sordida contemptae sortis amica iuvet!
quis Veneris famulae conubia liber inire
        tergaque complecti verbere secta velit?   (19–22)

The gods preserve me, if I had the urge to stray,
        from going after a girl of such mean station!
What free man would want to couple with a slave
        and embrace a back scarred by the whip?

If the ass, like the henpecked lover, can be pitied for his lot (*miserandae
sortis*, 7.15) then could not the slave (*contemptae sortis*, 7.20) as well?
Again, because of the assumptions he invites her to share, Ovid the lover
can be confident that Corinna (like the first-time reader) won't put two
and two together. The way that the reality of the slave's point of view may
be buried beneath the concerns of the free is indicated by the fact that the
lover has invited Corinna to see what is in front of her eyes (*aspice ut*

---

[32] In chapter 5 we will meet another long-eared ass/slave who overhears, namely
Apuleius' transformed Lucius.

auritus . . . asellus, 15) but she, like his readers, cannot see the familial figure of Cypassis for the familiar figure of speech. The beating that has disfigured the slave's back (22) is here a mark of degradation, not a form of treatment that might have consequences, as it is when the free man is figured as servile (16). But Ovid goes on to argue that he would be mad to solicit Cypassis, since the faithful maid would not only refuse him but betray him to her mistress (25–6). What are we to conclude from the fact that, evidently, she hasn't?

The dramatic effect of this diptych depends not only on the shocking juxtaposition of the oath that ends poem 7 with the bald revelation that begins poem 8, but also on the revelation that Cypassis has witnessed Ovid protesting that he would never stoop so low as to seduce a slave. Most scenes between a lover and his mistress at Rome would have been witnessed by a slave, maybe several, but that goes without saying. In these poems Ovid turns that inconsequential fact into a factor of the drama. The retrospective revelation of a presence in the first scene that has been apparently ignored by the interlocutors, a presence that both is and isn't part of the scene, can only remind the reader of his or her own presence. Like the maid, but unlike Corinna, the reader has passed from one scene (poem) to another and in doing so become, like Cypassis, a protagonist. To whom are *we* going to be loyal? It's too late; we've already taken Ovid's side without really hearing Corinna or seeing Cypassis, and so we're compromised ("What do you think of the way I brazened it out?").

Cypassis the hairdresser overlaps not only with the reader but, more obviously, with the poet, both as fellow artist and also as go-between. Doesn't the elegiac love-poet cast himself as facilitator of the love affairs of others?[33] Taking this one step further, we could say that just as Cypassis, in making her mistress beautiful to Ovid, commends herself as well as her mistress to him, so Ovid, making his beloved Corinna seem beautiful to his readers, commends himself to his readers as well as to her: the elegiac poet who claims that he has made his mistress famous is the same poet for whom the mistress is an advertisement (and symbol) of his own literary charms (*Am.*1.3.19–26). Cypassis is supreme in the art of arranging hair in a thousand different ways (*ponendis in mille modos perfecta capillis*, 8.1); Ovid's mastery is in a different art, but an

---

[33] Propertius 1.10.15–18.

65

art of *modi* (meters) just the same, and one could aptly say of this particular poet that his mastery, like hers, lies in the art of putting things a thousand different ways. Mediating the two arts is the art of love, which has its own *modi*, as Ovid remarks when he closes the second poem by threatening to reveal all: where they did it and how often and in how many different *ways* and which (*quoque loco tecum fuerim quotiensque, Cypassi, / narrabo dominae quotque quibusque modis*, 8.27–8). The poem is enclosed by the *modi* that link the surreptitious lovers both by association (as artists of *modi*) and by conjunction (the *modi* of their lovemaking). But Ovid's final threat makes a clear separation between them: if Corinna's relentless suspicions threatened, in the first poem, to turn Ovid into a beaten ass, for him to confirm them will sort out who is truly the slave, and for whom Corinna is truly the *domina*. In this diptych, Cypassis the slave serves as a presence about whom Ovid performs a dazzling play with the indirections, absences, substitutions, doublings and analogies that characterize poetry itself. The final lines make it quite clear who is their master.

If, like the love poet, Cypassis is the facilitator of other people's affairs, why should she not, like him, have her own? Indeed, how could she not? After all, how could the cook have the taste of the master, rather than a servile palate, if he had not been eating the master's food? Can the slave really be useful to the master or mistress without transgressing on the preserve of the free? If there is an "art" of love, then for Corinna to ask the slave to practice it on her behalf is to make of that slave a rival. Her beauty shines with the skill and labor of Cypassis, who knows how to make her mistress beautiful to her (Corinna's) lover. But in being suited to Corinna she is suitable *for* Ovid (*apta quidem dominae sed magis apta mihi*, 8.4), who knows her to be quite accomplished (*non rustica*, 8.3) on the evidence not only of his mistress's hair, but also of his "pleasant theft" (*iucundo . . . furto*, 8.3). The phrase "*non rustica*" acquires a technical, amatory sense of "not inexperienced in love" in addition to the more general sense ("sophisticated") appropriate to the hairdresser; at the same time, the word *furto* retains its original sense of "theft" under the erotic meaning ("affair") that is more common in Ovid's love poetry – Cypassis is Corinna's property, after all. The slave as go-between or facilitator is both extension and substitute, and what transpires across her ambiguous betweenness is the fluctuation between literal and metaphorical – in this case, lovers' jargon and the language of servitude. "It is enough to have serv(ic)ed (*emeruisse*, 8.24) *one* of your *dominis*" says Ovid, reassuring the nervous Cypassis with another *double entendre*.

In these two diptychs from the *Amores*, Ovid makes an issue of the betweenness of the slave: of the fluctuating nature of the slave's presence to the free; of the slave as third ear and other agenda; of the sliding of the slave's role between facilitator, supplement and substitute. This issue of the slave's betweenness is connected with a series of double meanings that invite us to see her presence in metapoetic terms. Poetry, especially ancient poetry, which is usually addressed to someone, has a double audience (here, Corinna and the reader), and this duplicity promotes the double meanings and wordplay that characterize the genre. What Ovid has done in *Amores* 2.7 and 8 is to conceive of this generic fact in dramatic terms, just as in 1.11 and 12 he has cast in dramatic terms the problem of how and what the written word communicates. It is the peculiar presence and status of the slave that precipitates these dramas.

Looking back, we can compare similar metapoetic dramas in Horace *Odes*.1.38, where issues of textuality and work are realized through the quarrel with an attendant slave, and in Plautus' *Pseudolus*, where the drama of being entertained by a theatrical performance is explored through the fictional machinations of a clever slave. Horace is concerned with the relation between the different kinds of work of poet and slave, Plautus with the relation between being entertained and being deceived by an underling. But in both cases something about the dynamics of the aesthetic is made visible by being diverted through the relationship between free and slave. The same could be said of Ovid, who is closer to Horace in his determination to align poetic mastery with the position of the master than to Plautus, whose analogy between playwright and slave has more subversive implications.

Ovid's Cypassis looks back to Horace's Davus, the listening satirist, and forward to the hero of Apuleius' *Golden Ass*, the focus of our attention in chapter 5. The bulk of Lucius' adventures take place while he is metamorphosed into a beast of burden, in which form he has access to all manner of secrets, and I will be arguing that Apuleius dramatizes the possibility of a certain kind of novelistic narrative through the figure of his hero's enslavement. All three of these enslaved figures, there and yet not there, have a presence that is comparable to some member of the literary dramatis personae (satirist, reader, omniscient narrrator). In chapter 5 I will be concerned not only with the enslaved protagonist as omniscient narrator but also with Apuleius' use of slavery as metaphor for a moral state; but before we turn to the *Golden Ass* I will consider some other uses of slavery as metaphor, and particularly its application to social, political and familial relationships.

CHAPTER

4

The continuum of (servile) relationships

As an extreme condition, slavery provided the free with a metaphor and a yardstick for a variety of relationships. Aristotle had mapped out political, social and familial relations in terms of dominance and subordination, drawing a series of analogies and distinctions between the different relationships, and others followed suit.[1] Cicero's version in *De republica* 3.37 (=Augustine *Contra Julianum*, 4.12.61) is particularly interesting:

> sed et imperandi et serviendi sunt dissimilitudines cognoscendae. Nam ut animus corpori dicitur imperare, dicitur etiam libidini, sed corpori ut rex civibus suis aut parens liberis, libidini autem ut servis dominus quod eam coercet et frangit . . . domini autem servos fatigant ut optima pars animi, id est sapientia, eiusdem animi vitiosas imbecillasque partes, ut libidines, ut iracundias, ut perturbationes ceteras . . .

> But the different kinds of ruling and serving should be distinguished. For as the mind is said to rule the body, it is also said to rule desire, but it rules the body as a king his citizens or a father his sons, but desire as a master his slaves, in that it restrains and crushes it . . . masters belabor their slaves as the best part of the mind, that is wisdom, does the flawed and weak parts of the same mind, such as desires, anger, and other disturbances . . .

Cicero identifies three spheres of domination: the state, the family and the individual. The slave-master relation takes its own place within these,

---

[1] *Politics* 1259a36–1259b16 and1260a8–15. Compare Sallust, *Cat*.1.2; Seneca, *Ben.* 3.18.3.

as a sub-category of familial relations, but slavery also provides a principle of differentiation: you can't dominate a citizen or a child as you would a slave; the body is to be guided, but the desires are to be compelled and chastened like slaves. Failure to observe these distinctions leads to slavish dispositions in the relevant sphere.

The third of Cicero's spheres, the individual, provided ancient writers with the material for a concept of natural slavishness. Those whose better parts were dominated by the worse, whose rational capacities served their appetites or passions, were slavish, and it would be in their interests to be dominated by those who could maintain the appropriate hierarchy within themselves.[2] But such naturally slavish people might occur anywhere, and this conception of natural slavery could not be neatly lined up with ancient practice in the way that belief in the natural slavishness of barbarians could (since only foreigners could be enslaved). The Stoics, who seem to have played a role in popularizing the doctrine that no man was a slave by nature,[3] made much of the distinction between legal slavery and true, moral slavery – that is, the incapacity for morally autonomous action on the part of those who were led by their lower selves. As Seneca puts it in his famous letter: "Show me who isn't a slave: some are slaves to sex, others to money, others to social prestige, all are slaves to hope and fear" (*Ep*.47.17; compare Epictetus, *Discourses* 4.1–40). Seneca also implies that the whole of society is a continuum of domination, a fact from which we must draw the moral consequences with respect to our behavior toward slaves: "Behave toward your inferior as you would want your superior to behave toward you" (*sic cum inferiore vivas quemadmodum tecum superiore velis vivere*, 11); and "Each time you remember how much you are entitled to do to your slave, you must remember also just how much your own master is entitled to do to you" (11). Others, as we shall see, could only regard such a continuum as a social scandal, a sign that things had gone wrong.

Another argument for natural slavery was the theory that in states where citizens are treated like slaves (monarchies, basically) the people will be slavish.[4] Such reasoning gave the democratic or republican states

---

[2] Garnsey (1996), 116–17.

[3] Garnsey (1996), 128. On slavery and the Stoics, see Manning (1989).

[4] Compare the Hippocratic *Airs, Waters and Places* 23.

of classical antiquity a rationale for their enslavement of foreigners. Some nations were "born for servitude" (see below, chapter 5) and Roman writers felt no compunction about casting the Roman empire itself as slavery.[5] But the end of the Republic and early Principate brought about the irony that the nation the gods intended to reign over all others was now itself in servitude to its political leaders.[6] As one might expect, during this period the metaphor of slavery acquired considerable currency in the political sphere; Cicero persistently speaks of existence under the triumvirs as servile.[7] In view of this currency, it is likely that the figure of Virgil's Tityrus, the slave who in *Eclogue* 1 goes to Rome to obtain freedom at the hands of a godlike young man, is conveying a political message and that Virgil is casting the propaganda of Octavian into a pastoral mode; after all, Augustus would open his *Res Gestae* with the claim that he had emancipated Rome from its servitude to a faction.[8]

"Servile" social relations

It is hardly surprising that slavery should so often be used to figure any situation that was felt to compromise the dignity or autarchy of the free citizen, since the opposition of slave and free played such an important role in the self-definition of the citizen. Theory demanded an absolute polarity between the autonomy of the citizen and the dependency and service of the slave, but in practice social relations might look more like a spectrum of dependencies and obligations.[9] Martial, intensely aware of the chain of dependency that characterized client-patron relations throughout Roman society, echoes Horace's Davus when he uses the

[5] *Aeneid* 1.283–5. In Tacitus' *Agricola,* the Caledonian chief Calgacus characterizes the Roman empire as the world's "ancient servitude" (*vetere famulatu,* 31.3). But contrast the Roman reaction to Prusias II of Bithynia's servility (Polybius 30.19 and Livy 45.44.19).

[6] For instance, Cicero *Phil.* 6.19 and 8.32. For Tacitus on the elite's *servitus,* see Wirszubski (1960), 160–7. The final blow was Domitian's assumption of the title *dominus et deus* (Suetonius *Dom.* 13.1).

[7] Dumont (1987) 635–87. For Sallust's use of servile metaphors, see Hock (1988). On Horace's *emancipatus feminae* (*Epode* 9.12) see Brophy (1975).

[8] Clausen (1994), 31–2. Servius on *Ecl.* 1.27–8 has a different interpretation of *libertas.*

[9] For a striking Greek version of the chain of "slavery" see Philemon, Fr. 31 K-A.

figure of the *vicarius* (slave of a slave) to make this point. While he dances attendance on Maximus, the latter does the same for another. "So we are equal," he says, concluding

> esse sat est servum, iam nolo vicarius esse.
>> qui rex est regem, Maxime, non habeat.   (2.18.7–8, cf. 2.32.7–8)

> It is enough to be a slave, I don't want to be a *vicarius* too.
>> The one who's boss, Maximus, shouldn't have a boss himself.

Publilius Syrus, himself a freedman, uses slavery as a metaphor for relations between the free in which an individual's autonomy might be compromised.[10] To call borrowing money "a bitter slavery for a freeborn man" (11) is perhaps not surprising, but to cast the normal reciprocities of Roman social life into the mold of slavery is more daring: to receive a *beneficium* is to sell one's freedom (61); to ask for a favor (*officium*) is slavery of a kind (641). The value attached to autonomy was so high that reality could never live up to ideal, and the ideology of mutual obligation could always be seen in a darker light. A word like *amicus*, which spanned a very wide range of relationships, both equal and unequal, served to mute any suggestions of servility in the rituals of attendance that characterized Rome's patronal society.[11] With an emperor at the apex of society, the social inequalities papered over by an ideology of mutual obligation became more pronounced. Horace's Davus, commenting on his master's reaction to a late invitation from Maecenas, no doubt voiced the worries of his master and creator. In another *Satire*, Horace has Teiresias give advice to Odysseus on how to reinstate his fortunes after his return home; in Odysseus' absence Ithaca has become contemporary Rome, where flattery and obsequiousness rule, and Teiresias' advice on the successful manipulation of prospective testators culminates with "Be the Davus of the comedies and stand with head bowed in simulated fear" (*Satires* 2.5.91–2).

As a number of scholars have observed, the language of the *servitium amoris* (slavery of love) featured by the elegists of the Augustan period overlaps with the language of patronage. The lover's fidelity, attendance, friendship (*amicitia*) and praise of his mistress all find their counterparts in the client's relation to the patron. Peter White, who remarks on the

---

[10] Christes (1979).   [11] Saller (1982), 11–15.

connections in language and behavior between the cult of the mistress and that of the poet's patrons, comments that it was natural for the elegists to describe the experiences of the young man in love by borrowing conventions from other forms of society poetry.[12] This is surely right as far as it goes, but it tells us little about the paradoxical, excessive character of the poet's flaunting of his *servitium*, the mixture of degradation and pride in the lover's stance. The poet-lover embraces the fact that the price of entry into his exclusive world of love is to leave behind his rightful freedom: "Now I see my servitude and a mistress readied for me: so now, farewell, my ancestral freedom" (*hic mihi servitium video dominamque paratam:/iam mihi, libertas illa paterna, vale*, Tibullus, 2.4.1–2).[13] What might be an anxious truth for the poet-courtier is a resigned, amused, or defiant acceptance of the rules of a game for the poet-lover, who serves as a lightning rod for all the floating dis-ease with the increasing servility of social relationships, collected into a bolt of lightning that strikes *this* extravagant figure. He becomes the object of a mixture of envy and pity because he has actively embraced what others find awkward and embarrassing. He clears the air. We could compare the poet-lover who boasts of his slavery to the comic slave who parades his physical punishment as a badge of honor. In both cases, the audience's pleasure in the character's disregard for the demands of dignity is compounded with the denial of some painful reality.

The embracing of a life of love, for which the poet-lover must acquire a range of servile attitudes that will stand him in good stead with his mistress, allows the poets to represent new kinds of potentially servile behavior in a form that is sufficiently remote and fictionalized to be harmless. In the middle of Tibullus 1.5, sandwiched between examples of the poet's servitude to his mistress (5–6; 61–6), is a fantasized idyll in which Tibullus and Delia entertain Messalla in their humble rustic abode, and Delia herself waits on the great man at table (*ipsa ministra*, 34). The connection is clear. Mario Labate has pertinent things to say apropos the social function of the *servitium amoris* in Ovid: "Ovid aims to create a precarious balance in which elegy is at the same time an exception (the parenthesis that can accommodate censored social behavior), and also

---

[12] White (1993), 87–91.

[13] Cf. Propertius 1.10.29–30. On the *servitium amoris*, see Copley (1947), Lyne (1979), Murgatroyd (1981) and McCarthy (1998).

the laboratory of behavior and experiences indispensable to modern social life."[14]

When Tibullus recommends to his mistress a poor lover, such as himself, he lists the services she can expect. They are the duties of a slave:

> pauper erit praesto tibi semper: pauper adibit
> > primus et in tenero fixus erit latere:
> pauper in angusto fidus comes agmine turbae
> > subicietque manus efficietque viam:
> pauper ad occultos furtim deducet amicos
> > vinclaque de niveo detrahet ipse pede.　　　　　(1.5.61–6)

> The poor man will always be there: the poor man will be the first
> > to visit you and will stick to your lovely side;
> the poor man will be a faithful companion in the crush of a crowd
> > and will take your arm and make way for you.
> The poor man will sneak you to secret lovers
> > and will himself loose the straps from your white foot.

The suggestive eroticism of this passage provides us with another example of the free person's fantasy of enslavement as a privileged position (cf. chapter 2). It is significant that the chains in the last line of the excerpt are not, as the context would lead us to expect, a metonym for Tibullus' own slavery (as in 1.1.55, 1.6.38, and 2.3.83–4), but rather his mistress's sandals. Perhaps *she* is the one who is enslaved by this display of servility.[15] This accords with McCarthy's argument that the love poet's attempt to win over and keep his mistress through servility reflects anxieties that masters will become dependent on their slaves.[16] She cites the passage in the *Ars Amatoria* (2.345–8) where Ovid recommends that the lover let his mistress grow accustomed to him by continual attendance, welcoming every trivial task (*taedia nulla fuge*, 346), until he can be certain that he will be asked for (*posse requiri*, 349) – at which point he should absent himself for a while. This method of achieving control by a strategic alternation of availability and absence plays off, and reveals, the masters' fears of becoming dependent on their slaves. Part

---

[14] Labate (1984), 174.
[15] Stephen Hinds suggests that the use of *ipse* (sometimes "the master") in line 66 colludes with this.　　　[16] McCarthy (1998), 179.

of the interest of a *topos* like the *servitium amoris* is that it may tell us as much about the psychology of slavery as about love: in order for a poet to cast himself in the role of the slave of his mistress he must draw on his own experience and imagination of the relation between himself and his slave.

Tibullus provides another example of this ironic connection between servility and control when he begs his mistress's husband to hand over his faithless wife to the poet-slave to chaperone: "but you could entrust her to me for safe keeping: I refuse neither cruel stripes nor chains on my feet" (*at mihi servandam credas: non saeva recuso / verbera, detrecto non ego vincla pedum*, 1.6.37–8.) Here it is the (slave-) guard Tibullus who is wearing the chains, an irony that recalls, in inverted form, that of the similar line in the previous poem, where the servile lover removes the "chains" from the foot of the mistress he serves (above). Similarly, in the first poem of the first book, Tibullus, contrasting himself with Messalla the military man, declares that he cannot accompany his patron on campaign because he is chained by love to his mistress and sits, a doorkeeper (*ianitor*), before her unrelenting doors (1.1.55–6). The *exclusus amator*, holding his lonely vigil, begins to look like the slave who stands guard over the very doors that are closed to the lover; but then the slave who might block the poet's access is himself excluded by his status from the kinds of access that the free man he excludes can attain. The paradoxical position of the slave, who had constant access (of a certain kind) to his master and mistress, and could be entrusted with the supervision or control of the free, acquires new figurative possibilities in the erotic context, and these are eagerly exploited by the love poets.

One of the most important of the citizen's freedoms was the freedom of speech, for which Greek had a special word ($\pi\alpha\rho\rho\eta\sigma\iota\alpha$). Slaves were normally required to curb their tongue (Seneca, *Ep.* 47.3), but on the most notable occasion that they were actually required to speak, their word could only be given under torture.[17] Not surprisingly, the subject of freedom of speech is raised by the love poets and, with the poet-lover a slave, judicial torture cannot be far away. Tibullus the lover is quite unashamedly prepared to relinquish his freedom of speech: in 1.5, after

---

[17] Watson (1987), 85–9 and Brunt (1980), on judicial torture at Rome. See also duBois (1991).

a rupture with Delia, he invites the torture that would be inflicted on a slave, but not to make him speak, rather to prevent the proud words that have precipitated the *contretemps*:

> ure ferum et torque, libeat ne dicere quicquam
> magnificum post haec: horrida verba doma.   (5–6)[18]

> Burn and torture this savage lover, remove his urge to speak
> proudly after this: control his rough words.

When Propertius the servile lover invites torture, he too alludes to the judicial torture of slaves in a paradoxical way:

> et vos qui sero lapsum revocatis, amici,
> quaerite non sani pectoris auxilia.
> fortiter et ferrum saevos patiemur et ignis,
> sit modo libertas quae velit ira loqui.   (1.1.25–8)

> But friends, who would recall, too late, your fallen friend,
> search out remedies for a mind diseased.
> I will bear the steel and fire with patience,
> let me only be free to speak what anger dictates.

There are two, possibly three, metaphors here, since steel and fire are the instruments both of surgery and of torture.[19] In connection with the previous line, Propertius' fortitude in line 27 appears as the stoicism of the patient submitting to the pain of an operation that will rid him of his malady. This he will gladly bear provided he can tell his story and express his anger freely. But the mention of *libertas* in the following line reminds us that steel and fire are also instruments of the judicial torture of slaves, applied to force out the truth about their masters and mistresses. Propertius, the "slave" of his mistress, enduring these tortures bravely, would be resisting the compulsion to bear witness against his mistress, but in the interests of exercising a free man's freedom to speak what his anger dictates. The implications of this very

---

[18] Cf. Tib. 1.9.21–2.

[19] Denis Feeney points out to me a third possibility, which is that the passage alludes to the gladiator's oath (*uri, vinciri ferroque necari*, Seneca, *Ep.*37.1). The lover commits himself to a willing slavery.

complex passage are hard to unpack precisely, but it seems that Propertius is paradoxically both acceding to and defying the demands of those who would have him betray his mistress; if he speaks, it will be on his own terms.

For the poet importuned by his patron to write, the freedom not to speak might be as precious as the freedom to speak. Horace's autobiographical *Epistles* are much concerned with freedom in all its dimensions, as Johnson (1993) has eloquently shown, and at the beginning of *Epistles* 2.2.1–25, excusing his failure to send the promised letter and poems (25) to Florus, Horace launches into a long parable about a slave dealer.[20] The dealer describes his merchandise as obedient, somewhat educated (*litterulis Graecis imbutus*, 7), versatile and tractable as soft clay, a boy who'll even sing pleasantly, though without sophistication, at a symposium. He has no need to exaggerate the boy's virtues, the dealer continues, because, unlike others of his profession, he's not desperate for a sale: he's poor, but he's solvent. In fact, the boy did once play truant, when he was hiding from punishment. You have no grounds for complaint if you buy the slave, comments Horace: the dealer has complied with the law (which obliged anyone selling a slave to report any defects). But I warned you, Florus, when you set out that I was lazy, and enfeebled when it comes to this kind of *officium*.

In this parable, Horace corresponds both to the slave (*litterulis Graecis imbutus*) and the dealer; he has split himself into the poet and the client who commends his services, and he has cast the whole transaction between patron and client into a framework that gently reminds Florus of the limits of the patron's rights over his client. Their relationship is as far removed as can be imagined from the dealings of the slave market, and yet there are awkward analogies that, Horace implies, need to be kept at bay. He makes his point with characteristic wit and delicacy, deploying comparisons that are ludicrous at the same time as apt. The profession of the slave-dealer (*mango*) being one of the most despised in Roman society, it is comically improbable for this one to profess a contented poverty (*meo sum pauper in aere*, 12), in the style of Horace's own persona. The very improbability draws attention to Horace's presence behind the mask at the same time as it mutes the reprimand with a laugh.

---

[20] On this passage, see Oliensis (1998), 7–13.

Family and slavery

In the passage with which this chapter opened, Cicero includes the family as one of the spheres of relations defined by dominance and subordination. The model of the family, revolving around the power of the *pater-familias*, was central to the conception of the Roman state, and *patria potestas* the prototype of Roman political authority.[21] As we have seen, the *familia* was a broader concept than our "family," and under the *pater-familias* the other members of the *familia* were all identified in some way as inferior, either by gender (wife), age (children) or legal status (slaves and freedmen). *Patria potestas* tended in theory to assimilate the various subordinates of the family to each other, so that all of the relations between members of the extended *familia* could be seen as modifications of that between master and slave.[22] But, as Cicero indicates, this tendency had to be resisted – sons could not be treated as slaves.

The Romans themselves regarded *patria potestas* as unique to them (Gaius, *Inst.* 1.54–5). The son, over whom the father legally had power of life and death, and who remained in his father's *potestas* as long as the father lived, had to be recognized at birth as a member of the household by his father; Wiedemann compares the slave, "saved" (*servatus*) in war.[23] Neither slave nor son owned property in their own right, and what assets the father allowed them to administer was called *peculium*. That the slave was called *puer* only accentuated the analogy.[24] Seneca, for instance, says "we must claim the right to bestow a benefit for slaves, that it may be claimed for sons also" (*vindicandumque ius beneficii dandi servis, ut filiis quoque vindicaretur, De Beneficiis* 3.29.1). Both slave and child were subject to corporal punishment. It is true, as Richard Saller observes, that there are plenty of statements distinguishing the kind of punishment the slave could expect (*verbera*) from those that the son might incur (*verba*).[25]

[21] Lacey (1986).

[22] But see the cautions in Saller (1996) on the distinctions between theory (legal or linguistic) and reality. Genovese (1972), 74, notes a similar tendency toward assimilation in the ante-bellum South.

[23] Wiedemann (1987), 22. On the dependence of the adult child, see Gardner (1993), 52–84.

[24] Aristophanes makes a revealing pun: "It's right to call someone who gets beaten *pais* (*paio*=beat), even when he's old" (*Wasps* 1297–8, cf. 1307).

[25] Saller (1994), 42–53.

A father could not treat his son like a slave in this crucial area; after all, the son was due in his turn to become a *paterfamilias*. But the fact remains that the son was not immune to corporal punishment, like adult free people, and the analogy with the slave was there to be made, even if, for that very reason, it had to be denied. In Plautus' *Bacchides*, for instance, the young man punished by a schoolmaster has "a hide as blotchy as a nurse's apron" (*corium tam maculosum quam est nutricis pallium*, 434), a type of expression often used about the punishment of slaves (see chapter 2). None of the structural analogies mean that fathers thought of sons, or treated them, like slaves; in fact, it is precisely the discrepancy between this structural or theoretical symmetry and the utter separation in reality between the two statuses that made the slave such a viable alibi for the son in the economy of the comic household, as we shall see.[26]

Relations between master and slave and between father and son are central to the comedy of Plautus, who overlaid the typical father-son domestic conflict of Greek New Comedy with a master-slave conflict.[27] Typically, the clever slave (*servus callidus*) sides with his young master against the *paterfamilias* in order to overcome the latter's real or potential obstruction of his son's amour. Parker (1989) sees in the trickster slave recruited by the young lover an alibi for the latter's rebellion against the father, whose authority stands in the way of his wishes. No wonder the slave Epidicus accuses the besotted young master who recruits his help of making his back into a substitute sacrifice (*succidaneum*) for his stupidity (*Epidicus* 139–40). The young master's transgressive love jeopardizes the slave's back, which is threatened with the punishment the *senex* will not inflict on his son, but in the end the slave is let off his punishment and his trickery usually achieves a desirable result: the girl in question turns out to be free, for instance. The *servus callidus*, as Parker has observed, is an inversion of the *paedagogus*, the slave/tutor who carries some of the authority of the father and bears the responsibility for keeping his ward on the straight and narrow. When the comic son makes himself over to the slave, becoming the slave of his slave, he reflects something of this paradoxically paternal role of the *paedagogus*, only now the slave's brief is to promote rather than restrain the desires of the

---

[26] On the use of the son-slave analogy and distinction in Christian authors, see Garnsey (1997).   [27] Anderson (1995), 178.

son against the restraint of the father.[28] Thus the slave is both an apotheosis of the son's rebelliousness and a parody by inversion of the father's guidance.

If there is a tension, inherent in the family, between the conserving role of the *paterfamilias* and the outgoing extravagance of the son, or between the son's duty to his family in the matter of marriage and his own unruly desires, it is the slave who embodies the rebellious aspects of the son's subordinate position. As a figure of sheer irresponsibility and playfulness, the slave insulates the family from the son's potential rebellion, and can do so by virtue of his ambiguous position within the household. His even-handed lack of deference to both father and son absorbs the sting of the war between them that is being waged through his medium and, as the amoral spirit of rebellious play incarnate, he provokes the adjustments between old and young, conservation and expense, that will eventually sustain the institution against which youth rebels.

Certain aspects of Roman marriage suggest analogies between slave and wife. In the early Roman marriage the wife passed into the *manus* (literally, "hand") of her husband, in some cases through a symbolic purchase (*coemptio*), though this form of marriage *cum manu* became rarer throughout the Republic; like the child and the freedman, the wife owed her husband *obsequium* (compliance).[29] In Plautus, the conventional distribution of power between husband and wife is sometimes challenged by the figure of the *uxor dotata*, the heiress whose property gives her independence of her (often henpecked) husband.[30] Part of the wife's property would comprise her slaves, and these might play a role in promoting the wife's interests in household politics. In the *Asinaria*, for instance, Demaenetus, trying to get round his wife, finds that he must deal with her servant Saurea, and when his own slave Libanus points out that the slave in question is more in his wife's power than his own (84–6), Demaenetus replies by underlining the fact that the proper state of affairs has gone awry: "I took the money. I sold my authority for a dowry" (*argentum accepi, dote imperium vendidi*, 87).

---

[28] A *paida-par-agogos*, in Parker's pun; as he points out, the only slave who actually is a *paidagogos* (Lydus in *Bacchides*) functions as a blocking character. Parker (1989), 243.

[29] Treggiari (1991), 16–36 and 238–41. On marriage and slavery, see Joshel and Murnaghan (1998), 4.   [30] Rei (1998), 95–9.

As McCarthy (forthcoming) shows in detail, Plautine comedy explores the ironies of domination and control, meditating on them through the central institution of slavery, which becomes the reference point for other relationships. Not all of the comedies feature a *servus callidus*. Parasites, prostitutes, and philandering *patresfamilias* can also hold the position of rebel or trickster, but when they do they allude to the figure of the slave. The *Menaechmi*, for instance, features a parasite, Peniculus ("Brush"), so called because when he eats he wipes down the table (78). Aligning parasitism with servility, he makes the point that those who bind captives with chains and put shackles on runaway slaves have got it wrong: if you want to prevent someone from running away you should bind them to you with food and drink. No chains are stronger (79– 97).

Casina is Plautus' most complex dramatization of the network of domination and subordination in the *familia*, and it will concern us for the rest of this chapter.[31] The plot plays fast and loose with the normal distribution of roles:[32] both father and son are in love with the same slave, the eponymous Casina, who is owned and has been brought up by Cleustrata, the *matrona* (45–6). One can still see the outlines of a traditional structure in which young love triumphs and is rewarded with marriage, a storyline that was probably followed by the Greek original, for Plautus tells us in the prologue that Casina will turn out to be the neighbor's daughter and will marry the son of the household, Euthynicus. But Plautus' play does not end with a marriage, nor does it actually feature a young lover, and Lysidamus' son is kept out of the way. The prologue announces, with glorious disregard for illusion, that the playwright has broken the bridge to the city by which he was to pass (65–6). The play focuses, instead, on the *senex amator*, Lysidamus, who schemes to marry off Casina to his bailiff, Olympio, so as to have free access to her himself. The intrigue, in which Lysidamus's scheme is foiled by an alliance of women and slaves, is familiar from modern comedies such as *The Merry Wives of Windsor* (and Verdi's *Falstaff*), *Der Rosenkavalier* and *The Marriage of Figaro*. Like them, it ends with an elaborate trick humiliating the would-be philanderer.

---

[31] Rei (1998), 99–104 and McCarthy (forthcoming) are both excellent treatments of *Casina* in this context.

[32] Well analyzed by McCarthy (forthcoming).

Lysidamus, the *senex amator*, takes up the role of the scheming rebel usually played by the slave; it is he who deploys military language to describe his plans in the manner of the *servus callidus* (307–8, 344, 352).[33] The blocking function is now played by his wife, Cleustrata, who has elements of the *uxor dotata*. But even this redistribution of roles is unstable, because Lysidamus is still the *paterfamilias*, holding official power in the household, and Cleustrata, together with her friend and neighbor Myrrhina, must resort to concocting a scheme to frustrate his plans. She too appropriates the role of the clever slave, and the women use the kind of metatheatrical language about their plot that normally comes from the mouth of the slave protagonist. Where the prototypical Plautine comedy features a slave who casts himself as a general, politician, or aristocrat in his plot against the *paterfamilias*, this one features free people who claim the position of the *servus callidus* in rebellion against their familial role.

Accompanying these appropriations of the role of the slave by the free characters are the alliances that the protagonists strike with slaves in order to further their schemes. The household is both a collection of analogical master-slave relations and a web of intrigues and alliances carried out by the free through slaves; in Jakobson's terms, the master-slave relation has both metaphorical and metonymical dimensions.[34] Lysidamus has commissioned (*adlegavit*, 52) his *vilicus* (bailiff) as a front for his pursuit of Casina, and the son has commissioned his arms-bearer. Both promote their proxies as candidates for the hand of Casina. As soon as he realized that his son was a rival, Lysidamus sent him abroad (*ablegavit*, 62), but his wife, Cleustrata, has taken their son's side and supports him in his absence.

After the prologue setting the scene, the play opens with a familiar wrangle between town and country slave.[35] Chalinus and Olympio seem oblivious to the fact that they are proxies for their masters, and argue over the hand of Casina. Olympio the *vilicus*, as master of his domain, threatens to torment the *armiger* when he gets him on his own territory, while the *armiger* mocks Olympio as the country slave who is out of his depth in town. The first confrontation between Lysidamus and Cleustrata will mirror the altercation between the two slaves: where the

---

[33] On Lysidamus as the *servus callidus*, see McCarthy (forthcoming).

[34] Jakobson and Halle (1971), 90–6.

[35] Compare the first scene of the *Mostellaria*.

slaves seem oblivious of their status as proxies of father and son, husband and wife speak as if the matter had to do with the slaves. Neither of them is fooled.

The following scene introduces Cleustrata as mistress of the household, countermanding Lysidamus' orders that lunch be served: the larder is to be locked and the key returned to her. She berates her absent husband with imputations typical of Plautine slaves insulting each other (158–60). Like Olympio the bailiff, Cleustrata has power within her own realm, in spite of her subordinate status. Olympio has his *praefectura* (99, 110; cf. *provinciam*, 103), the country estate in which, in the master's absence, he is all-powerful, while Cleustrata claims for herself the *curatio* (258ff.) of the maids, deploying, like Olympio, a term of political office.[36] She protests to Lysidamus that he should leave his wife to her domain and Lysidamus seems to agree, ruefully, that Cleustrata has *imperium* in the house (409). When, in a later scene, he tries to reassure an edgy Olympio that his own power, like Jupiter's, is absolute, Olympio is not convinced. He knows that he cannot afford to alienate the other members of the household; supposing this human Jove were to die, and his rule revert to those minor gods? (330–6) Cleustrata will play Juno to Lysidamus' Jupiter (405–8) and spoil his amatory fun.

Lysidamus' first entry picks up on the previous scene where his wife makes arrangements to deprive him of lunch. He still has food on his mind, but only in a manner of speaking. The song with which he introduces himself praises love as the most effective of spices. Why, then, is it the only one that cooks don't use? It has even transformed Lysidamus himself from a grumpy *senex* into an elegant sophisticate (*lepidum et lenem*, 223). Throughout the play, food and love will exclude each other (as he will later say, "he who loves neither hungers nor thirsts," 795) and here Lysidamus's comparison situates them on separate levels of reality as one becomes a metaphor for the other. This is his implicit response to his wife's control of the larder, and the resultant division between wife and husband is a modified version of a conventional routine between master and slave that crops up twice in this play: when Lysidamus asks him "What's up?" Olympio responds "You're in love and I'm suffering from hunger and thirst" (725, repeated at 801–3).[37] One might compare the similar distribution in the prologue to *Poenulus* (discussed above in

[36] *OLD* 4a. [37] Compare Aristophanes *Ploutos*, 190–1.

chapter 2), where the audience must satisfy itself with *fabulae* while the slaves make for the cakeshops. Here, Olympio's comeback both contrasts and compares: Lysidamus lives off love, and so is satisfied (795, 801ff.), but love is also the master's high-class version of hunger and thirst, and won't be satisfied (cf. 809–10). When the women, together with their allied slaves, sabotage the wedding feast for Olympio and Casina with endless delays (772–5), Lysidamus, true to his word, tells them to go ahead with the feast without him; he will eat later at the country estate with bride and groom (780–7). For Lysidamus, love comes first, but not for the women. Pardalisca the maid comments that the two women are waiting for her master to leave so that they can swell their own bellies undisturbed (*ventris distendant suos*, 777). The suggestion of pregnancy in this phrase intimates that, for them, food substitutes for sex.

In the end, Lysidamus will be deprived even of his sexual satisfaction by the alliance that controls the kitchen, and Chalinus alludes to his role in the deception of Lysidamus by adapting his master's culinary metaphor:

> ibo intro, ut id quod alius condivit cocus,
> ego nunc vicissim ut alio pacto condiam,
> quo id quoi paratum est ut paratum ne siet
> sietque ei paratum quod paratum non erat.   (511–14)

> I'll go in and change the seasoning
> of what's been seasoned by another chef,
> so the preparation's not prepared for whom it was
> and what was not prepared for the other one now is.

The master may have the advantage of living on a higher plane, but those who control the mechanics of the household can see to it that he must live on metaphor alone. Their satisfactions are more solid and, in the end, his love becomes a *form* of hunger. In *Casina*, Plautus has expanded the slave's conventional "You're in love and I'm hungry" into a nuanced exploration of relations of power and status within the household, cutting across the division of slave and free.

Slavery and marriage are again brought into the same orbit in the scene where Olympio delivers to his master the good news that Casina will be his to enjoy that night. Olympio describes himself with adjectives conventionally given to wives (*obsequens*, 449 and *morigerus*, 463). As it turns out, Lysidamus' proxy in this betrayal of his wife may also have served as substitute for her: his master's grateful welcome becomes increasingly warm, even erotic, until Olympio cries out "get away from my back" (*apage a dorso meo*, 459), leading the eavesdropping Chalinus to conclude that Olympio has earned his position as *vilicus* by sexual compliance; he adds that Lysidamus once tried to make him "door-keeper" at the front door itself. Here grateful affection slides into sexual abuse and the *senex amator*'s pursuit of the slave Casina takes on a more sinister tone; as McCarthy (forthcoming) points out, the scene also recalls Lysidamus's wheedling attempts, earlier, to mollify his wife with affectionate advances, which she rudely rebuffed (230–5). Again, the chain of sexual exploitation and manipulation runs through both slave and free.

In the denouement of the play, Cleustrata and her allies arrange to substitute the disguised Chalinus for Casina in Olympio's wedding cere-mony, and as the "bride" approaches Pardalisca, parodying the ceremo-nial advice of the *pronuba,* urges him/her to get the upper hand in their marriage: let the husband keep "her" in clothes while she strips and despoils him (821–2).[38] This division of labor corresponds to the masters' version of slavery, according to which the master provides for the slave while the thieving slave plunders him.[39] In Pardalisca's song, slavery and marriage are implicitly compared as conditions where the subordinate is both parasite and insurgent.

The revolt of the subordinates succeeds. Lysidamus, discovered and humiliated, realizes that the game is up (937ff.). He must go in to his wife and offer up his back for the insult he has inflicted on her. Perhaps someone in the audience would like to take his place? No? Then his only hope is to flee like a runaway slave – there's no chance for his shoulders if he returns (949–56). Not only does Lysidamus acknowledge that the balance of power has shifted, but he reaches to embrace the role of comic slave as the only resource available to him; stepping into the realm of metatheater, he appeals to the laws of the genre. When Cleustrata enters, he throws himself on her mercy, promising never to behave like this again, on pain of being hung up and beaten by his wife (1001–3). Having

[38] Parody: Rei (1998), 101.

[39] Seneca, *Tranq.* 8.8. Compare Chalinus here (293): *liber si sim, meo periclo vivam, nunc vivo tuo.*

become the generic comic slave, he must, by the laws of the genre, be for-
given, and so Myrrhina urges. Cleustrata agrees, also stepping into the
metatheatrical dimension – she will not make the play any longer than it
already is (1004–6). So Lysidamus, having initially tried to use his slave
as an alibi for his own lust, and failed, is finally reduced to playing the
slave himself in order to take advantage of the sympathetic rebel's immunity.

Lysidamus' strategy bears some relation to that deployed by the
poet/lover of elegy. In both cases servility is affected in order to manipulate one who temporarily has the upper hand. The next chapter will deal
with some of the imaginative ramifications of the possibility that a free
man might truly become a slave, rather than just adopt that mask. Here
too we will see that, in the imagination of the free, the slave has certain
advantages. But the real possibility of enslavement is shadowed, and
mitigated, by a discourse of moral "slavery," which brings us to the third
of Cicero's spheres of metaphorical slavery, the individual.

CHAPTER

5

Enslavement and metamorphosis

In the previous chapter we have seen that the polar opposition between slave and free coexisted with a spectrum of relations haunted, to varying degrees, with the specter of servility. Another factor that troubled the theoretically absolute separation beween slave and free was the traffic between the two states, apparently so separate: slaves were continually being freed and a number of circumstances could reduce a freeborn person to slavery. In this chapter, then, we will look at enslavement and (briefly) emancipation, the crossings of the great divide beween slave and free.

From slave to free

The impression given by the surviving records is that manumission was common among domestic slaves, but this impression may be misleading; for one thing, the epigraphic record is probably unrepresentative and, for another, the ideal represented by Roman authors that manumission was the expected reward of faithful service may be just that, an ideal.[1] Nevertheless, freedmen are ubiquitous in the surviving literary and epigraphic corpus and the Greeks at least regarded Roman practices as remarkable.[2] The formally manumitted slave at Rome took on the status of his master, which meant that, unlike Athens (where the freed slave became a metic), Rome accepted freed slaves into the citizen body.[3] The freed slave retained obligations toward his or her original owner as well as

---

[1] The cautions are Wiedemann's (1985); Hopkins (1978), 115–18 puts the case for frequent manumission.

[2] Dionysius of Halicarnassus *Antiquitates Romanae* 4.22.4–23.7.

[3] On manumission, see above, intro.n.12. On freedmen, see Treggiari (1969), Fabre (1981), Andreau (1993).

certain legal disabilities, and inhabited legally, socially and morally, an in-between world.[4] For the freedman or freedwoman, freed status might be a source of pride: Petronius' Trimalchio and his freedman friends insist on their self-made, independent status (*Satyricon* 57, 75–6), and in this they recall the freedmen *advocati* of Plautus' *Poenulus* (515–28 and 533–40), determined to assert their respectability and self-sufficiency.[5] The similar characterization suggests that we are dealing with a literary stereotype. But among their new fellow citizens the freedmen's slave past remained a stigma.[6] Horace claimed to have been haunted by the jingle "born of a freedman father" (*libertino patre natum*, *Satires*.1.6.6, 45, 46 and *Epistles* 1.20.20) and the freedman Phaedrus evidently felt it necessary to preempt such prejudice by attacking social confusion in his *Fables*.[7] Furthermore, as a figure who was often the business agent of a more powerful freeborn person, the freedman might be the more visible (and safer) target of the resentment of the freeborn poor.[8] Petronius' millionaire freedman Trimalchio, the ancestor of many of modern literature's *nouveaux riches*, presents us with a man obsessed, appropriately, with illusion, transformation and puns, several on the word *liber* (*Sat.* 41).[9] His banquet is an exercise in metamorphosis, where everything turns into something else. As his chef makes meat out of pastry, he makes mincemeat of Greek mythology and behaves with the randomness of Fortune itself. He is an anomaly in the world of the free, and the house of this hybrid, as Bodel (1994) has demonstrated, is imagined as a social underworld.

From free to slave

But what about those who made the passage in the opposite direction? To what extent did a freeborn person who was enslaved become servile and to what extent did he or she remain a hybrid?

---

[4] Veyne (1961) and (1988), 72–84, which argues that freedwomen provided the milieu in which we are to imagine the elegiac lovers pursuing their affairs.

[5] On freedmen in Roman comedy, see Rawson (1993), and on freedwomen, Veyne (1988), 75–7 (re *Cistellaria* 22–41).

[6] Martial 2.29 has a freedman covering up the *stigma* on his forehead with plasters.

[7] Bloomer (1997), 73–109.

[8] Joshel (1992) 128–31 makes a convincing argument that this is what lies behind Juvenal's attacks on freedmen.

[9] *Trimalchio at West Egg* was Scott Fitzgerald's original title for *The Great Gatsby*; Bodel (1994), 256 n.37.

Ancient thought made a closer identification between the person and the circumstances of life than we do, but some writers claimed that there were people (even nations) who were by nature slavish, whether or not they were slaves.[10] The problem was that it was hard to claim that such people, and only such people, had become or been born as slaves. The theoretical distinction between natural and legal slavery, together with the realities of enslavement and emancipation, raised a number of problems, and not only for philosophers. Aristotle, of course, was troubled by contradictions stemming from the fact that "naturally" free people could be enslaved by the fortunes of war,[11] but a freedman's epitaph from Narbo seems to be written with an eye to this same issue. "I, to whom a barbarian land gave birth, was delivered by custom into undeserving slavery, so that my character was changed" (*barbara quem genuit tellus, hunc tradidit usus / servitio, ingenium ut flecteret, immerito*).[12] Perhaps the identification of his birthplace as barbarian alludes to statements about the natural slavery of certain races, but the writer emphasizes that it was *usus*, not nature, that made him a slave, and undeservedly. Far from claiming, as for instance do some of Euripides' characters,[13] that he retained a free spirit in his new circumstances, he acknowledges that servitude altered his native character; since *ingenium* echoes *genuit*, he may be insisting that a man becomes servile by circumstance, not by birth.

The same freedman prides himself on the fact that he has been a good slave, who won over his master by services and did not suffer the whip (*officiis vicit dominum nec verbera sensit*, 5). But is not the concept of the good slave something of a paradox if servility itself is a moral failing? Might the recalcitrant slave not be exhibiting a laudably free spirit? Seneca raises this very possibility: "How vile to hate someone you should praise – and how much more vile to hate someone for something because of which he deserves to be pitied; namely because as a captive who has suddenly fallen into slavery he holds on to some remnants of his former free status and fails to hurry to perform sordid and difficult services" (*De Ira* 3.29).

Seneca speaks for the slave as one who has a story rather than just a status, and speaks with some empathy of what it means to be enslaved.

[10] On theories of natural slavery, see de Ste Croix (1981), 416–18. For nations born for slavery, see Cicero, *Prov. Cons.* 10 (*Iudaeis et Syris*); Livy, 35.49.8 (*Suros omnes*) and 36.17.5 (*Suri et Asiatici Graeci*) and Lucan 4.575–9.

[11] Garnsey (1996), 75–8.   [12] *CIL* 12.5026, see Eck and Heinrichs (1993), 24–5.

[13] For example, *Helen* 728–33 and *Ion* 854–6.

As a Stoic, he prided himself on anticipating mentally whatever fortune might have in store, and enslavement was the limit of possibility in this respect. But how often did the Roman master who looked at a slave see himself, but for the grace of God? In the *Iliad*, the "day of slavery" hangs over the women of Troy continually, and in *The Trojan Women* of Euripides and Seneca that day arrives, bringing the pathetic spectacle of noble women facing the prospect of ignominious slavery to the slayers of their husbands and sons.[14] The wars that brought foreign captives to Rome also made Roman citizens prisoners of war, and every soldier knew that defeat might mean slavery. Etymology reminded him of this fact: according to Florentinus (*Digest* 1.5.4.2), slaves are called *servi* because generals sell their prisoners rather than killing them, and thus preserve (*servare*) them, and they are called *mancipia* because they are captives in the hands (*manus*) of their enemies. Roman law regarded a captured Roman as a slave, though the right of *postliminium* enabled him to recover citizenship retrospectively on his return; if he died in captivity, however, he died a slave.[15]

Some of the more traumatic defeats of Roman history brought the possibility of enslavement into vivid focus and gave a new meaning to the presence of the slave: "You are as able to recognize a free man in him (the slave) as he is a slave in you. After the destruction of Varus' army fortune cast down many people of glorious birth, making one of them a shepherd, another the doorkeeper of a hut . . . Go ahead, despise a man whose fortune is one into which you can pass yourself, for all your contempt" (Seneca *Ep*.47.10). The defeat at Carrhae was another profoundly traumatic event for the Romans, a puncturing of the illusion that only foreigners could be slaves, and in his "Regulus Ode" (*Odes*.3.5) Horace conjures up the disgrace of Roman soldiers captured by the Parthians at Carrhae living with barbarian wives and in-laws. He recalls the advice of Regulus, the captive Roman general sent back by the Carthaginians to negotiate terms of peace during the First Punic War: Roman captives should not be ransomed from Carthage, Regulus urged; having chosen life in captivity over death, they have lost their *virtus* and it cannot be redeemed. What of Regulus himself, then? Though he also had survived to become a captive, he was, in effect,

---

[14] On slavery in Euripides' Trojan plays, see Rabinowitz (1998).

[15] Watson (1987), 19–21.

choosing death when he gave this message and returned to face torture and execution at the hand of his captors, true to his word. The poem fades out on a scene of intense pathos as Regulus, acknowledging his servile status (*ut capitis minor*, 42), refuses the kiss of his wife and children. He becomes the preeminent Roman *exemplum* of nobility and heroism by accepting enslavement, though he will not live to endure the same condition as his soldiers. This paradoxical hero/slave is a dead man, and being dead he is already an *exemplum*, not a slave, a substitute for the more disturbing reality of the Roman soldiers who have changed their very being.

Between the unbowed Regulus and the captives from Carrhae, willing members of an alien community, there is the third category of those who have survived to become members of the very class they most despised. Only philosophy offered comfort for this eventuality: "the body is enslaved, not the mind" (Seneca, *Ben*.3.20). As ancient philosophy became increasingly concerned with the self abstracted from its political, social and familial embedding – a "true" self – slavery was seen as the limit case of a circumstance in which the true ethical core of a human could be preserved against the surrounding world. Several of the great post-classical philosophers had themselves been slaves (and some were simply reputed to have been), the Stoic Epictetus among them. When it comes to propounding the crucial doctrine that we should resign ourselves to what is not within our control, Epictetus (*Dis*.4.1.76–9) uses the metaphor of slavery: the body, subject to circumstances we cannot control and "a slave to everything that is stronger," should be voluntarily resigned to its slavery. "You ought to treat your whole body like a poor loaded-down donkey . . . and if it be commandeered and a soldier lay hold of it, let it go, do not resist or grumble. If you do, you will get a beating and lose your little donkey all the same."[16]

For the Stoics, legal slavery was an external circumstance that left the true self untouched; but the corollary was a true, ethical slavery, into which even the legally free might fall.[17] One of the most famous of Stoic

---

[16] The figure of the beast of burden as slave will concern us when we come to Apuleius' *Golden Ass*, which, as it happens, contains an episode in which Lucius the ass is commandeered by a soldier from his master (9.39–40).

[17] For the Stoics on slavery, see Manning (1989) and Garnsey (1996), 128–52.

paradoxes was "Only the wise man is free." Philo, the Hellenized and Stoicizing Jew, wrote two paired works titled "Every Good Man is Free" and "Every Bad Man is a Slave" (the latter is lost). An association, going back to the Athenians, between freedom and self-control, or slavery and incontinence, was available not only as a justification of slavery – it is in the interests of the one who cannot control himself to be ruled by the one who can – but also as a metaphor for the ethical life.[18] But to say that a free man could become enslaved in this way (to passions, greed, lust, etc.) is not necessarily to claim any affinity between slave and free. In fact, it serves to separate those who live in the realm of metaphor from those who are tied to literal meanings. Occasionally, though, this metaphorical discourse on slavery comes into contact with the realities of living with slaves, as for instance in the anecdotes about philosophers beating slaves, where philosophical self-control is dramatized in terms of an ethical issue that has to do with the treatment of slaves: anger threatens to make a "slave" of the master who beats his slave. Another such case is Seneca's famous letter (47), where practical suggestions about the benefit of living on terms of familiarity with slaves are interwoven with reflections on the vulnerability of all to fortune, on the continuum of servile relations and on the existence of an ethical slavery to which even, or particularly, the rich and powerful are susceptible. However, Seneca's potentially disturb-ing initial reflection that we are all vulnerable to fortune, and therefore *conservi* to our slaves, is mitigated by the reassuring final complaint that masters who are quick to anger against their slaves behave like kings who take offense (*quasi iniuriam accceperint*) at an underling, *forgetting* the huge disparity in strength and fortune between them: "We assume the temper of kings; for they too, forgetting both their own strength and the weakness of others, flare up and rage, as if they had received an injury, though the magnitude of their condition renders them completely invul-nerable to such a threat" (*Ep.*47.20).

Another case of the interaction between metaphorical discourse about ethical "slavery" and issues of living with slaves is Apuleius' *Golden Ass*.[19] The hero, Lucius, is led by a "slavish" curiosity into making ill-advised

---

[18] Just (1985).

[19] For a different reading of the *Golden Ass* in terms of slavery, see Gianotti (1986). Thebert (1993), 142–4 has an interesting account of the information about slavery to be gleaned from this work.

experiments with magic, which result in his being turned into an ass, stolen by bandits and forced to undergo a succession of painful servitudes. An extraordinary first-person narrative about the experience of servitude as a beast of burden is framed by philosophical and religious metaphors of slavery. Apuleius' novel combines a narrative of moral fall and religious conversion, for which enslavement is the primary metaphor, with a collection of curiosities and voyeuristic observations, to which the position of the servile beast of burden provides the crucial access.[20]

Enslavement, servitude and the novel

The motifs of exposure, kidnapping and abduction by pirates are among the most maligned of literary plot devices, but ancient comedy and the novel would be unthinkable without them. They allow the characters and readers to get out and see the world, moving us from one locale to another; they provide the thrill of sudden changes of status, as well as the steady menace of a fickle fortune, and they engineer extraordinary recognitions and paradoxical encounters. *Apollonius of Tyre*, for instance, features a confrontation between a father and his daughter, now a prostitute, in which neither realizes the other's true identity. An implausible near miss? Perhaps not, since several theologians of the early Church advance as an argument against visiting brothels the possibility that a father might unwittingly have intercourse with a son or a daughter, a fact that prompted John Boswell to embark on his study of the abandonment of children from antiquity to the Renaissance. Boswell argues that these creaky plot devices may well reflect reality no less (or more) than American crime entertainment does.[21] The possibility of free people being enslaved in one of these "literary" ways was real, but a happy ending was allowed by the fact that, at least until the time of Constantine, Roman law regarded freeborn status as inalienable in these circumstances, even in the case of parental abandonment.[22] In the ancient novel, no one falls irrevocably into the orbit of slavery, and the gravitational field of freedom maintains a constant pull.

The early European novel gives servants almost as important a role as that of the enslaved hero or heroine in the ancient novel, and the mediat-

---

[20] On *Golden Ass* see Winkler (1985), Schlam (1992) and Shumate (1996).
[21] Boswell (1988), 98.   [22] Boswell (1988), 70ff.

ing work in this respect is Apuleius' *Golden Ass*. The connection was made by Bakhtin, who identified the type of the "adventure novel of everyday life," featuring a rogue or adventurer who does not occupy any fixed place but passes through everyday life and is forced to study its workings.[23] In this type, of which the Picaresque is the main example, "servants replace the ass." The hero of the anonymous *Lazarillo de Tormes*, for instance, passes from master to master just like Apuleius' Lucius. With the servant as hero, we are given access to all classes and a chance to spy or eavesdrop on the most intimate aspects of life. Since a novel is an inside story, the perspective of the novel will often be that of the servant in the house.[24] But the servant as hero or heroine also provides for a story of social mobility: Richardson's enormously popular and influential *Pamela*, whose heroine successfully resists the designs of her master on her virtue (like the heroines of the Greek romantic novel), and is eventually rewarded with marriage, is a good example. Apuleius' Lucius, as we shall see, is rewarded for his tribulations with a very particular kind of elevation, but the figure of the upwardly mobile slave was a not uncommon feature of ancient literature; there was, for instance, a tradition that Cyrus began as a slave to Astyages and worked his way up by diligence to become Persian emperor, and one of the kings of Rome, Servius Tullius, was believed to have been born a slave.[25]

The *Golden Ass* and the alienated body

First, a brief synopsis of the work. Lucius, a young, educated Greek, is passing through Thessaly on business, eager to experience at first hand the fabled magic of the area. The wife of his host in Hypata conveniently turns out to be a witch. Lucius decides that he will acquire access to the secrets of his hostess's art by seducing the maid Fotis, who turns out to be a compliant and skillful partner, and eventually she agrees to let him watch her mistress at her secret arts. Lucius sees her turning herself into a bird but, trying to repeat the transformation himself, he takes the wrong magic potion and ends up as an ass. Almost immediately he is stolen by bandits and undergoes terrible sufferings at their hands as a beast of burden. He passes from owner to owner, witnessing and hearing many

[23] Bakhtin (1981), 124–5. [24] Levin (1966), 37.
[25] Martin (1990), 35–42 and 49–50. Compare Seneca, *Troades* 887, *profuit multis capi.*

fascinating and titillating stories, and suffers unbelievable cruelties from those for whom he works. Finally he is transformed back into a man at a festival of Isis and becomes a devotee of the goddess, ending up in Rome as a successful lawyer, proudly displaying the shaven head of the Isiac.

The *Golden Ass* is similar in outline to the basic plot of the Greek romantic novel, a story of deracination and restoration.[26] But in the Greek novel the main driving force of the plot is love: the enslavement that compounds the separation of the young lovers threatens the chastity that guarantees a true restoration of the lovers to each other. Of course, the threat is (almost) always withstood. This emphasis on the preservation of chastity corresponds to the philosophers' concern with the integrity of the ethical self in the face of slavery, guaranteeing that the protagonists remain essentially free through their servile episodes. But there is a more tangible sign of the true nobility of the lovers, namely the beauty that sets them apart from their fellows and cannot be alienated even by enslavement. As a character in Chariton puts it, "It is impossible for a body to be beautiful which is not by nature free" (2.1.5). Achilles Tatius' Leucippe, chained, shaved, filthy and miserably clothed, "shouts" her noble origins through a beauty that remains undiminished by her degrading circumstances (5.17.4).[27] Lucius' enslavement, by contrast, is precipitated by a metamorphosis that not only robs him of his physical beauty but gives him a body that is made for work.[28]

The enslaved heroes and heroines of the Greek novel are still the same people under their changed circumstances – only their relation to power has changed. Their adventures as slaves are a testing ground for the qualities (some of them physical) that will prove they deserve the status with which they were born. But Lucius' asinine body not only prevents him from communicating, and totally changes the nature of his presence among humans, it also brings with it "asinine" thoughts and behavior. Lucius is concerned about the extent of his transformation, and intent on proving that he still has a human mind and human appetites. He is a hybrid, sometimes like the proverbial slave with a free spirit, sometimes like the barbarian freedman whose nature was changed by enslavement.

[26] But see Stephens and Winkler (1995), 3–5 on the possibly unrepresentative nature of the surviving "big five" romantic novels.

[27] Cf. Longus, *Daphnis and Chloe* 4.17.

[28] Aristotle, *Politics* 1254b, maintains that nature wanted to make the bodies of slaves fitted for the work they perform.

It is never quite clear where the boundary between his human and his asinine identity is to be drawn.

For others, Lucius is a being whose existence counts for nothing more than the work that can be extracted from his body, and he must hear his owners discussing whether he is still worth the price of his upkeep, knowing that when this ceases to be the case he may be killed.[29] This alienation from his own body is given an ironic twist when Lucius contemplates running away from the bandits, but asks himself who would give shelter to a mere ass? But this is an asinine thought, he immediately counters, for who would not be glad to take his own means of transport (*vectorem*) with him (6.26)? The thought is asinine (human for "foolish") because Lucius is still thinking in terms of his former status, and its loss, not in terms of his new form and its use for others, which has certain advantages for him.

The body of the ass has at least one feature that will be a source of pleasure, both to Lucius and to us, namely longer and more acutely sensitive ears. Where the Greek novel tends to begin with the pleasures of the eye, in two cases an elaborate *ecphrasis* (*Daphnis and Chloe* and *Leucippe and Cleitophon*), *Golden Ass* promises from the start to tickle our ears (*auresque tuas benivolas lepido susurro permulceam*, 1.1), and its narrative is constantly suspended by inserted tales.[30] Once he has been transformed, Lucius will have access to the intriguing tales that will soothe the ears of us readers by virtue, in part, of the longer, more sensitive ears of the beast that he has become. But it is not only the anatomy of the ass that will let the narrator exercise his own curiosity and satisfy ours, it is also the status of the beast of burden as chattel. Lucius remarks that people are not shy of freely doing and saying whatever they want in front of him, since now they take little account of his presence (9.13).

So, both the body of the beast of burden and his negligible status provide us with access to titillating stories. In the prologue, the narrator refers to his style of writing with an equestrian metaphor, calling it a *desultoria scientia* (the skill of a rider jumping from horse to horse). This image of authorial omniscience, and of the story's easy passage between widely divergent milieux and levels of reality, is certainly apt in a book about an ass. But it gets things quite the wrong way round, since our nar-

---

[29] 6.26; 7.20; 7.22–3.

[30] On *ecphrasis* and the visual in the Greek novel, see Bartsch (1989).

rator/hero, far from jumping from one horse to another, is a beast of burden who gets around by lending his back to one owner after another – the reverse of the *desultor* who leaps from back to back, in other words. Ironically, the very mobility and omniscience of the narrator derives from the powerlessness and inconsequentiality of the hero as chattel. In fact, Lucius' metamorphosis produces an inversion of the phrase *desultoria scientia*, for just as there is a knowledge that the *desultor* manifests, so there is a knowledge that comes from inhabiting the reverse position, for which there is no name, a knowledge that wells up from the subconscious of a slave-owning society. Horace's anxiety at what the slave may know, manifested in his ventriloquizing of the slave Davus as a form of conscience, is now replaced by a *curiosity* for what the slave knows, a desire to hear him tell his tale and report what he has seen.

Alienated from his own body, Lucius is a parody of the Greek romantic heroines, whose beauty triumphs wherever they go, though not necessarily to their advantage. Everybody wants them, and that is the problem. Apuleius invites us to reflect on the parallels and contrasts between these two kinds of alienation from a body that is essentially *for* others by embedding into Lucius' story the tale of Psyche, whose beauty is so transcendent that it reaps her no benefit (4.32). She hates what pleases others in her (4.32), and eventually the renown of her beauty incurs the jealousy of Venus.[31] Psyche, like Lucius, is both downwardly and upwardly mobile: she is condemned by the order of a jealous Venus to conceive a passion for the lowest of men, but Cupid, charged with carrying out Venus' punishment, falls in love with her and substitutes himself. As a result of her curiosity she loses Cupid and is reduced to the status of a runaway slave of Venus (6.8);[32] but, after suffering maltreatment as a member of the *familia* of Venus, she is promoted to a legitimate marriage with a member of the Olympian family. The beautiful Psyche is the mirror image of the deformed Lucius, but what is most significant for the novel's imaginative world is the structural nexus, in both of their stories, between the alienated body, deracination and social mobility. Both characters, in a sense, lose the ownership of their bodies, from which they receive only suffering; both are taken away from their world and sink to

---

[31] The tale of Psyche is itself embedded in the narrative of Charite, a figure straight out of the Greek romantic novel. Charite has been abducted on her wedding day by the same brigands who stole Lucius, and will later be saved by her fiancé.

[32] Echoing Moschus' *Eros Drapetas*; Kenney (1990), 190.

the level of slaves, and both end up in a new and socially desirable position. Venus herself reminds us of the slave's potential mobility when she threatens to adopt one of her own home-born slaves (*vernulae*) into Cupid's position as a punishment for his betrayal (5.29). Whatever the allegorical implications of these two stories as spiritual progresses, it is slavery that provides the terms through which these transformations can be imagined.[33]

If Lucius the beast of burden bears a structural relation to the beautiful heroines of the Greek novel, he is also an inversion of a figure that appears several times in the novel, namely the traveler, whether merchant or tourist. Lucius himself is passing through Thessaly on unspecified business, but Aristomenes and Socrates in the first tale of the book are merchants. All three of them are diverted from their purpose, and all, except Lucius, fail to return home after they fall foul of witchcraft. The same is true of Thelyphron in Book 2, who sets out to see the Olympic Games, but takes a diversion to visit the infamous Thessaly and arrives at Larissa broke; trying to earn some easy money, he falls prey to local witchcraft and ends up so disfigured that he can never return home. Socrates, we learn, was returning from a successful business trip when he took a diversion in order to see a show and fell into the clutches of a witch. He ends up dead. The merchant is, in some respects, a mirror image of the slave: the former detaches himself from his community to make profit from his mobility, whereas the slave, by virtue of his deracination, is human merchandise that passes from hand to hand and can be claimed by any purchaser. One might say that the community through which the merchant passes is vulnerable to his mobility, whereas the deracinated slave is available to the community that incorporates him. But the position of the opportunistic traveler is precarious and can easily be reversed. Lucius himself intends to combine business with pleasure and sample the local Thessalian speciality, magic. What transpires, however, is that through the operations of magic he becomes a scapegoat for the community of Hypata in their annual festival of *Risus* (Laughter). Having served as the ritual object of laughter in the community's festival, Lucius is offered (or threatened with) permanent memorialization in the form of a statue (3.11); in other words, his desire to be a transient con-

---

[33] For a different view of the relation between Lucius and Psyche, see Penwill (1975) 50–9. On Cupid and Psyche as allegory, see Kenney (1990).

sumer of the exotic product of Thessaly is thwarted when Hypata uses him to serve its ritual purposes and threatens to freeze him permanently in this role. The opportunistic journey of the deracinated merchant or tourist puts his status in a precarious position, dangerously analogous to that of the slave if his project goes awry and he becomes the exploited rather than the exploiter. This precariousness is the context of Lucius' metamorphosis into a chattel and beast of burden: he tries to turn himself into a bird (which Columella uses as a figure for the merchant)[34] but instead becomes an ass (a common figure for a slave).[35]

Animals and slaves

Clearly Apuleius has contaminated the novelistic plot of deracination and restoration with the animal fable, and it is an intriguing possibility that this may be the one literary genre in the ancient world that preserves traces of a fiction produced by slaves.[36] The two famous fabulists of antiquity, Aesop and Phaedrus, were both freed slaves (on the historicity of Aesop see above p. 26, n. 28), and Phaedrus actually attributes the invention of the fable to the fact that slaves, liable to punishment for any offense, had to find ways of disguising what they could not say outright (3 *Prologue*, 33–7). Many of these fables reflect the bitterly resigned outlook of an underclass that has little hope of deliverance from its sufferings.[37] So it may be that slaves appropriated the animal status assigned to them by the official culture of their masters as a position from which to voice their own perspective.

Apuleius' contemporary, Artemidorus, says that in dreams animals used for humble tasks symbolize laborers and subalterns (4.56), and that to dream of having an ass's ears or head signifies slavery and misery (1.24 and 37). The rationale for this symbolism is that the domestic animal and

---

[34] *De Re Rustica*, *Praef.*1.8.4.

[35] An interesting example of this is the graffito from the Palatine *paedagogium* in which a drawing of a burdened ass is accompanied by the words "Work, ass, as I have worked, and it will be to your advantage." Eck and Heinrichs (1993), 102.

[36] Bradley (1987), 150–3 makes a cautious argument that "fables were at least influenced by forms of slave protest-statements."

[37] Compare the Uncle Remus stories collected by Joel Chandler Harris (on which, see Flusche 1975). Bloomer (1997), 73–109 interprets Phaedrus' *Fables* from the perspective of his freedman status.

the slave both inhabit an ambiguous place in the ancient system of categories. In the Aristotelian scheme, domestic animals inhabit the highest layer of the category of the infra-human, next to slaves and barbarians, who occupy the lowest layer of the human.[38] Greek and Roman law shows a fluid boundary between the domestic animal and the human, whose space is often shared with these animals.[39] In Greek, slaves are referred to collectively as *andrapoda* (human-footed), by analogy with *tetrapoda* (four-footed), and ancient texts frequently associate the domestic beast and the slave.[40] The *Golden Ass* makes this connection several times: for instance, Lucius refers to his horse as his *famulus* (3.26), to whom he becomes, after his transformation, a *conservum* (7.3); the auctioneer who is selling him makes labored, but unwittingly apposite, jokes about whether the ass is of free origin (8.25); after his restoration, Lucius dreams of the return of his slave *Candidus*, who turns out to be his white horse (11.20) .

Like the slave, the ass is the animal that is beaten. When the metamorphosed Lucius becomes an ass he exchanges his skin for a hide (*corium*). The Latin word not only denotes a type of body, it also connotes a particular relation of one body to the will or uses of another. For instance, the phrase *corium petere* ("to seek the hide") means "to ask for someone [almost always a slave] to be flogged"; as one might expect, the word is common in Plautus. More broadly, the proverbial "*de corio suo ludere*" means "to risk one's own skin" (*Golden Ass* 7.11) and to do something "*de corio alicuius*" is do it at another's expense (*panem de meo parabat corio*, *Golden Ass* 7.15). Throughout his adventures as an ass Lucius suffers cruel, even murderous, beatings, which he describes in lavish detail; these descriptions fluctuate in tone between the incredulous horror of the newly enslaved – Lucius tells us that his skin is as sensitive as before (6.26) – and the humorous detachment of Plautine gallows humor (7.17 and 7.18). Not only is his body persistently used and abused by others, but even in speaking about it himself, Lucius often treats it as an alien object.

The brutal cruelty of many of Apuleius' episodes is anticipated in Phaedrus' fable "The Ass and the Priests of Cybele" (4.1), which bears a

[38] Garnsey (1996), 110–14.
[39] Gianotti (1986), 22–4 and Mélèze-Modrzejewski (1975), 95–6, 99–100.
[40] Finley (1980), 99, Gianotti (1986), 23–4 and Thebert (1993), 139.

resemblance to one of Lucius' adventures. In Phaedrus' fable the ass that has been worked and beaten to death by the priests is skinned and his hide is used to make a drum. When they are asked what has happened to their favorite (*delicio*), the priests reply "he thought he'd be safe after death, but, look, new blows are rained on him now he's dead." Lucius himself is sold, in Book 8, to a band of itinerant Galli of dubious sexual proclivities under whom he suffers a murderous beating for "betraying" their secret orgies with his bray.

A less brutal attitude to the inescapable fate of the exploited is taken by Aesop's fable about the ass and the gardener (Perry, *Aesopica: Fabulae,*179), which belongs to the abundant ancient literature on the vanity of human wishes. An ass belonging to a poor gardener asks the gods for deliverance from his sufferings. Hermes is sent to have the ass sold to a potter, but the animal's hardships are worse than ever under his new master. The story repeats itself, with each master worse than the previous one in a sadistic spiral that, like the Fable of the Ass and the Priests of Cybele, captures something of the flavor of Apuleius' narrative. The moral of the story, that slaves miss their old masters only when they get to know the new ones, is hardly revolutionary. Whatever their origins, by the time these fables were collected in their literary form they reflected a range of perspectives, with that of the masters prevailing. Lucius himself speaks of his sufferings as an ass with a mixture of self-pity and righteous satisfaction, expressing both the outrage of the newly enslaved and the detached amusement of the master. Those who expect his experiences at the hands of his fellow humans to provoke reflections on social injustice will be disappointed.

Some of Phaedrus' fables do seem to speak from the perspective of the slave, even if the appended morals make their application more universal, and therefore less subversive.[41] Most notable in this respect is the story of the ass and the old man (1.15). A timid old man kept an ass in his meadow. Terrified by the sudden cry of enemies approaching he urged the ass to flee with him and escape capture. "Will they load me with two packsaddles instead of one?" the ass asked. "Of course not," the old man replied. "Then what difference does it make to me whom I serve?" The universalizing moral that precedes the story gives it a political slant ("in

---

[41] The story of the ass and the Galli, for instance, has the rather bland moral that the one born unlucky is pursued by Fate even after death.

a change of government [*principatus*] the poor change nothing but the name of their master"), but the separate worlds of slave and master, so near and yet so far, could hardly be more succinctly described, nor the irony of the slave's perspective more pungently expressed. In a similar scene from the *Golden Ass* (6.28–30), Lucius bears Charite as they both flee the bandits who have abducted them. In this case, animal and human share the same interests, but when they come to a crossroads Lucius the ass is unable to convey to Charite that the direction she has chosen is the one from which the bandits will be returning from their exploits; he stubbornly resists her guidance and the struggle between rider and stubborn ass ends in their recapture. As in Phaedrus' fable, Apuleius' irony here derives from the fact that horse and rider are so near and yet so far.

Curiosity and "slavishness"[42]

In view of the bizarre turn that Lucius' life will take, it is significant that the narrative of *Golden Ass* begins with Lucius dismounting from his horse:

> I was riding a native-bred pure white horse; as he too was now quite tired, and in order also to dispel my own weariness from sitting by the stimulation of walking, I jumped down to my feet. I carefully rubbed the sweat from my horse's forehead, caressed his ears, unfastened his bridle, and led him along slowly at a gentle pace.
>
> (1.2)[43]

In another book this would hardly be an event, but as the beginning to this particular story it acquires unusual prominence, for Lucius the ass will have reason to wish that all humans would treat their mounts with such consideration, and he will bitterly recall his care for the horse when stabled with it in his asinine form. More importantly, as Apuleius phrases it, the episode describes Lucius changing his extension: separating himself from the horse, marked as a lower form of being by the word *pronus*,[44] Lucius makes himself a third to two humans. One of these travelers has just told the other an extraordinary tale of witchcraft and murder, and Lucius joins

---

[42] The bibliography on *curiositas* in *Golden Ass* is extensive. See Schlam (1992) 48–66; Penwill (1975); De Filippo (1990); and Hijmans (1995).

[43] Translation of Hanson (1996).   [44] See the uses cited in *OLD* 3b.

the conversation as the other protests that the tale is incredible. He displays for the first time the curiosity that will lead to his own metamorphosis into a beast of burden as he urges the storyteller to repeat his tale: "Please let me share your conversation. Not that I am inquisitive (*curiosum*), but I am the sort that wants to know everything, or at least most things" (1.2). But before this first conspicuous occurrence of the *Leitmotif* of Lucius' adventures there has been another use of the term that goes unnoticed in treatments of this theme: Lucius *carefully* wipes the sweat from his horse's brow (*equi sudorem frontem* curiose *effrico*).[45] This care requires an imaginative identification with the tired body of the horse that is, in a sense, metamorphic – Lucius will later come to know all, or at least most, of what it means to be an exhausted beast of burden. The usage indicates both sympathetic projection into the sensorium of another and the paternalistic relation between owner and chattel that has no independent status. In one sense the horse is an extension of Lucius' own body, and in another it is the epitome of the non-human. When the tale of his new travelling companion is finished, Lucius thanks the teller for lightening the burden of the journey, adding that his horse must also be grateful, since he has ridden all this way to the city gate of Hypata not on the horse's back, but on his own ears (*non dorso illius sed meis auribus pervecto*, 1.20). Here is a more benign version of the comic symbiosis between slave and master represented by Plautine exchanges such as: (master) "I'm in love" (slave) "My shoulders feel it" (*Poenulus* 153).

But if this story of metamorphosis explores the curious fact that horse and rider (slave and master), those two different orders of being, are in some sense one body, it also carries the antidote to that awkward realization, namely an allegorical narrative in which slavery is a metaphor for a moral state into which the free might fall. At its loftiest level the novel bears a philosophical or moralizing narrative of transgression and punishment that focuses on the consequences of Lucius' "slavish" behavior. This allegorical reading of the *Golden Ass* is encouraged by the words of the priest of Isis:

> "You have endured many different toils and been driven by Fortune's great tempests and mighty stormwinds; but finally, Lucius, you have reached the harbour of peace and the altar of Mercy. Not your

---

[45] It is not, for instance, in the list of Hijmans (1995), 364–5. For a similar collocation of *curiositas* and *curiose*, see 6.21, where Cupid carefully wipes the sleep off Psyche and then castigates her for her curiosity.

birth, nor even your position, nor even your fine education has been
of any help whatever to you; but on the slippery path of headlong
youth you plunged into slavish pleasures and reaped the perverse
reward of your ill-starred curiosity." (11.15)[46]

"Slavish pleasures" alludes to the sensual delights that Lucius enjoyed
with Fotis, and since she was herself a slave the phrase is overdetermined.
In ancient thought, pleasure is slavish both because it tends to sap the
self-control that is characteristic of the free spirit and because pleasure is
purveyed by slaves. The same double determination applies to Lucius'
trademark sin of curiosity, which both manifests a "slavish" lack of self-
control and is a trait attributed to slaves.[47] Could we go further and say
that Lucius' story displays curiosity *about* the slave? Certainly his all-con-
suming curiosity leads him to find out what it is to be on the bottom of
the heap, but is Lucius, or indeed any ancient person, actually curious
about the experience of a slave? Conveniently, Plutarch, to whom the
fictional Lucius claims to be related (1.2 and 2.3), wrote a treatise about
curiositas (*De Curiositate*), and in that work he uses the relation between
slave and master as a figure for the proper relation between reason and
the senses in connection with curiosity:

But, as I think, the faculty of vision should not be spinning about
outside of us, like an ill-trained servant-girl, but when it is sent on
an errand by the soul it should quickly reach its destination and
deliver its message, then return again in good order within the
governance of the reason and heed its command. (521 C)[48]

According to this philosophical framework, Lucius' sin would be that he
has allowed a desire that should only be auxiliary – a curiosity serving,
motivating the rational – to become a principle of action in its own right.
His metamorphosis into an ass is a punishment that fits the crime by
making him live the life of a partial being *as though* it were a complete
one, that is, with the consciousness of a free human. In Plutarch,
πολυπραγμοσύνη (*curiositas*) is treated as a disease that infects people
with the desire to know about the ills and misfortunes of others, a form

---

[46] Translation of Hanson (1996).
[47] Sandy (1974) argues that the priest's "slavish pleasures" specifically applies to
Lucius' desire to meddle with magic.
[48] On Plutarch and Apuleius, see Walsh (1981).

of *Schadenfreude* that seems to allow busybodies to confirm their own sense of security by feasting their eyes on the weaknesses, misfortunes and failings of others. But the only case where Plutarch suggests that curiosity about the experience of another might actually motivate a desire to take the other's place is where he describes adultery as curiosity about another's pleasure (519 C)!

In the *Golden Ass*, Lucius' experience of slavery seems to be the ironic result, or punishment, of a free-ranging but irresistible curiosity. His metamorphosis is the reductio ad absurdum of his wayward desire to experience otherness, as well as the appropriate result of his forfeiting of the freedom that comes from self-control; the control that he has lost must now be exerted over him by others. Within this framework, the experience of the slave cannot be conceived as a proper object of curiosity. In fact, we might, somewhat anachronistically, describe the allegorical or philosophical structure of the narrative as one that *precludes* curiosity about the experience of the enslaved: Plutarch's comparison of the curious to the slave girl implies that curiosity, being itself slavish, cannot have slavery as its object.

One of the reasons why curiosity is a slavish characteristic is that the domestic slave is privy to a great deal that the master, or mistress, would rather remained hidden. The proverbial *curiositas* of the slave simply scapegoats the slave for the knowledge that has been thrust upon him.[49] Lucius the listening ass might well stand for the slave (compare Ovid's Cypassis poems); in fact, in Lucian's *Lucius, or the Ass*, possibly an epitome of Apuleius' source, the protagonist decides to try to gain access to his hostess's magic through the maid Palaestra because "Slaves know everything, good or bad" (5).[50] Significantly, one of the very few occasions on which we hear about Lucius' own slaves in the *Golden Ass* is when Fotis takes the precaution of laying their beds as far as possible outside the door of his bedroom "to banish them from supervision (*arbitrio*) of our nocturnal chatter, I imagine" (2.15). Much later in the book we are on the other side of this little scene, with Lucius the ass spying on, and exposing, the adulteries that transpire in the house of the baker.[51]

---

[49] Spying slaves: Aristophanes, *Frogs* 752–3; Martial 11.38 and 12.24.

[50] On the problem of Apuleius' Greek source, see the summary in Schlam (1992), 22–5.

[51] For voyeuristic slaves, see Martial 11.104.13–14.

It is worth taking a closer look at the episode of the baker's wife, since its embedded tale of Philesitherus and Arete features a slave, Myrmex. The embedded tale and its frame between them contrast the reassuringly servile Myrmex with the resentful slave represented by the asinine Lucius. The baker's wife complains to her confidante that her lackluster lover is frightened even by the face of "that mangy ass" (9.22); though he doesn't know it, the lover has good reason to be frightened, since the cruelty of the baker's wife has sharpened Lucius' curiosity about her exploits (9.15). Lucius eventually takes his revenge, exposing the adultery of the baker's wife to her husband. But by now she has a different lover, for her confidante has awakened her interest in the young Philesitherus by recounting a tale of his resourcefulness as adulterer, the story of Philesitherus and Arete, wife of a certain Barbarus. In this tale Myrmex the slave is charged by Barbarus to watch over his wife while he is away on a business trip. Myrmex ("ant") is everything a slave is expected to be: terrified, witless and easily corruptible. It doesn't take long for Philesitherus to play off Myrmex's greed against his fear and acquire access to Arete. When Barbarus returns unexpectedly, Philesitherus barely escapes being caught *in flagrante*, but leaves his shoes behind in the panic of the moment; the shoes arouse Barbarus' suspicion and he drags Myrmex off to the Forum in chains, searching for the shoes' owner. But Philesitherus' quick wit saves the day. Seeing the unfortunate Myrmex weeping and wailing, he accuses him of stealing his shoes at the baths. Myrmex is pardoned and all is as it should be: the husband has been cuckolded and duped; the slave has been corrupted and then saved by the resourceful Philesitherus. Here is the slave who can be relied upon, in his weakness, to do what suits the interests of the protagonist, on whom he then depends for salvation. However, the frame of the story, in which Lucius exposes the adultery of his mistress, is about the revenge of the enslaved, whose transgression is motivated not by greed, which would make him pliable to the intentions of the free, but by resentment. The unsettling presence of the silent, resentful slave is represented here by the disturbing face of the ass that scares the prospective adulterer.

From maid to goddess

Curiosity is connected closely by the priest of Isis with the *serviles volup-tates* that allude to Lucius' dalliance with Fotis. The motives of sexual pleasure and curiosity are, in fact, intertwined, for the seduction of Fotis is a means of access to her mistress's magic arts. Pamphile herself, being the wife of his host, and a witch, is too dangerous a woman to deal with directly, and so Lucius approaches her through the maid. As it turns out, Fotis is attractive, playful and sharp and Lucius has already detected a flirtatiousness in the way she tucks him up in bed. But it is the sight of her working in the kitchen that really fires his lust.

In the Victorian household it was the spectacle of the maid kneeling on all fours and scrubbing that seems to have awakened the fantasies of the upper-class male. Stallybrass and White (1986), 153–4, remark on the irony of the fact that the position of the maid on all fours awakens desires of bestial copulation in the master while the servant is performing the very work that maintains the propriety of the bourgeois household. The bourgeois household is contaminated by beings who are dirty because they clean, beings from whose circle the child must be detached in the process of becoming proper, and who then become objects of forbidden desire. Desire for slaves was not usually regarded as perverse in the ancient world, though when it was stigmatized the image that recurred was that of the back scarred by the whip: Ovid brushes off Corinna's accusations with a protest that he would hardly embrace a back that had been whipped, and the perverse tastes of Tacitus' Messallina (*Annals* 11.36.1–2) and of the lovely Circe in Petronius' *Satyricon* (126) are indicated in the same way. But in general, the slave, being a person who catered to the pleasures of the free, was regarded as an appropriate object of pleasure, as well as a subject given to pleasure.[52] How far from the kneeling maid is the sight of the working Fotis that awakens Lucius' lust when he comes upon her in the kitchen mixing sausage-stuffing, her whole body undulating as she stirs the pot!

> ipsa linea tunica mundule amicta et russea fasceola praenitente
> altiuscule sub ipsas papillas succinctula, illud cibarium vasculum
> floridis palmulis rotabat in circulum, et in orbis flexibus crebra
> succutiens et simul membra sua leniter illubricans, lumbis sensim
> vibrantibus, spinam mobilem quatiens placide decenter undabat. isto
> aspectu defixus obstupui et mirabundus steti; steterunt et membra
> quae iacebant ante. et tandem ad illam "quam pulchre quamque

---

[52] On sexual relations between the free and the slave, see Kolendo (1981).

festive," inquam, "Fotis mea, ollulam istam cum natibus intorques!
quam mellitum pulmentum apparas! felix et certius beatus, cui
permiseris illuc digitum intingere."

   tunc illa, lepida alioquin et dicacula puella: "discede," inquit
"miselle, quam procul a meo foculo, discede. nam si te vel modice
meus igniculus afflaverit, ureris intime nec ullus exstinguet ardorem
tuum nisi ego, quae dulce condiens et ollam et lectulum suave
quatere novi."   (2.7)

   She herself was neatly dressed in a linen tunic with a bright little
red band tied high under her breasts. She was turning the pot
around and around with her flower-like hands, shaking it often in a
circular motion, and at the same time she undulated gently, with a
slight wiggle of the hips, swaying her agile back so that her body
rippled softly. I was transfixed by the sight, utterly stunned. I stood
in amazement, as did a part of me which had been lying limp before.
Finally I spoke. "How gorgeously, my Fotis," I said, "and how
delightfully you twist your little pot with your buttocks! What a delicious stew you are cooking! A man would be lucky – surely even
blessed – if you would let him dip his finger in there."

   Then she, with her wit and her ready tongue, retorted: "Get away,
poor boy; get as far away as you can from my oven, because if my
little flame should blow against you even slightly, you will burn deep
inside and no one will be able to extinguish your fire except me. I can
season things deliciously, and I know how to shake a pot and a bed
to your equal delight."[53]

The eroticism of this scene is not flavored by the thrill of the forbidden
or the piquancy of degradation; rather, the undulations of Fotis as she
prepares the succulent mixture seem to reconcile work with sensuality
and to align all the senses in happy agreement. Her skill at awakening the
appetites of the free is treated, facetiously, as a source of power. This
idyllic scene is recalled towards the end of the book, at the nadir of
Lucius' fortunes, when he is working at the mill. After an exhausting day's
work, Lucius postpones his dinner to take stock of the scene around him,
which he observes "not without pleasure." This time he is gazing at the
servile working body from the other end of the social ladder, for these

---

[53] Translation of Hanson (1996).

slaves are actually above him in status. The sight is a hideous parody of the vision of Fotis in the kitchen, her limbs showing voluptuously through her clothes as she works, her breasts accented by a red band:

> dii boni, quales illi homunculi vibicibus lividis totam cutem depicti, dorsum plagosum scissili centunculo magis inumbrati quam obtecti, nonnulli exiguo tegili tantum modo pubem iniecti, cuncti tamen sic tunicati ut essent per pannulos manifesti . . . (9.12)

> Great gods, what pathetic specimens of men, painted all over their skin with livid weals, their beaten backs more shaded than covered by a torn cloth, some wearing a short covering reaching only to the privates, but all dressed in such a way that they were visible through their rags.

For the animals, work at the mill is an endless circle as they turn the wheels that will grind the grain into the flour that will find its way into kitchens where Fotises prepare meals under the appreciative gaze of Luciuses. The circular motion of the wheels they drive grotesquely echoes the undulations of Fotis as she stirs the pot. When Lucius the ass is hooded and installed in the channel of the largest of the mill wheels, the language verges on allegory:

> . . . et ilico velata facie propellor ad incurva spatia flexuosi canalis, ut in orbe termini circumfluentis reciproco gressu mea recalcans vestigia vagarer errore certo. (9.11)

> My head was covered and I was immediately given a push along the curved track of a circular channel. Within an orbit circumscribed all round, ever going back over my own path, I retraced my very footsteps and wandered on an invariable course.

Here the horror of the free man at the prospect of this drudgery is expressed by the pleonastic circumlocution of the language, which seems to stutter over the empty repetitiousness of the labor; as it does so, this cruel parody of a journey becomes a metaphor for a life that has gone astray. For Lucius the temporary beast, the paradoxical phrase *errore certo* (literally, "definite wandering") expresses both the senseless monotony of the labor that is demanded of him as an ass and, from the perspective of the final book, the comforting presence of Isis, the unexpected goal of the wanderings imposed on him by a blind Fortune. Confronted with the terrible reality of work at the mill, the free imagination takes refuge in allegory, an allegory that refuses the reality with which it is confronted.

Hoping that he will be thought unfit for this type of work and given a less oppressive task, Lucius the ass stands rooted before his millwheel in feigned stupidity. But his "ruinous cleverness" (*sollertiam damnosam*, 9.11) is to no avail, for several of the mill-hands surround the hooded ass with sticks and, at a given signal, shout and lay into him with such violence that he abandons his plan and leans eagerly into his work. Lucius concludes the episode with the words "I excited the whole company to laughter by my sudden change of philosophy" (*subita sectae commutatione*) (9.12). The phrase *subita sectae commutatio* is a grim joke, expressing the cruel satisfaction of the master at the fact that the slave must eventually recognize his lack of choice. But Lucius eventually does undergo a "change of *secta*," whose suddenness might well appear comic. After his escape from the arena at Corinth he falls asleep on the beach, but in the middle of the night he wakes in sudden fright, sees the moon and, convinced that all things are ruled by her majesty, decides to pray to her for deliverance (11.1). This is the beginning of the lengthy process of his initiation which finally takes him to Rome, where the story ends with Lucius the successful lawyer proudly displaying the shaven head of the Isiac. The terrified beast of burden's recognition of its subordination at the mill is echoed by the similar recognition on the beach, and the one episode both naturalizes and compensates for the other. Lucius, it is implied, can no more evade his conversion to Isis than can the ass resist his "conversion" to servitude; but, at the same time, voluntary slavery to the goddess occludes any other form of slavery. The free person's appropriation of slavery as a metaphor serves to exorcize the specter of real enslavement. In the *Golden Ass*, the shift from literal to metaphorical slavery performs the same kind of ideological function as does the physical distinction of the beautiful protagonists of the Greek novel from their fellow slaves.

Lucius' "conversion" to servitude at the mill ends with a telling shift of perspective when the mill-hands laugh at his "sudden change of philosophy." Their laughter deflects attention from the cruelty of the situation, and from the unthinkable prospect of a free man confronting a life of labor as a slave, to the satisfying and comic reliability of animal, or servile, nature. The metamorphosed Lucius is neither human nor animal, but he is also both; his double perspective allows him to convert horror at the cruelty of the master into satisfied laughter at the impossibility of an animal escaping the demands of its owners. Living with the enslavement of other human beings requires precisely this mobility of imagination from the free: the specter of one's own possible enslavement mirrored in a fellow human must be deflected by the reassurance that the slave cannot resist his or her condition, an impossibility which has to be rehearsed again and again so as to confirm the impermeability of the barrier between slave and free. Lucius, both human and animal, is the vehicle for this double consciousness which, borrowing the narrator's metaphor, we might call "desultory" (*desultoria*).[54] His hybridity is not only a moral metaphor for the lower and higher selves but also the site where anxieties caused by the *presence* of slaves in human society are enacted and negotiated.

Slave of the deity: from Isis to Jesus

The trajectory of Lucius' adventures in the *Golden Ass* could be described as the passage from one kind of voluntary and metaphorical slavery to another: Fotis and Lucius, making the *servitium amoris* mutual, protest to each other that they are bound together by a slavery they freely accept (2.10 and 3.19); similarly, the priest of Isis urges Lucius to commit himself to the servitude of the goddess (11.15), "for as soon as you become the goddess's slave, you will experience more fully the fruit of your freedom." To be the slave of a slave, of course, is shameful, and expresses in social terms the degradation of Lucius' moral servitude to pleasure, whose consequences were servitude of a more literal kind. The priest of Isis offers Lucius freedom from the sway of Fortune, but a freedom that is only attained through a new kind of servitude: the goddess has emancipated him *into* slavery – *in servitium . . . vindicavit*, a reversal of the common expression for emancipation, *in libertatem vindicare*. Lucius' story ends not with the restoration that is typical for the Greek novel but with a further episode in the story of his transformation and servitude. He is still a slave, but the slave of a goddess; he has been

---

[54] Compare the "double-consciousness" described by Du Bois (1997), 38 as the legacy of slavery to the African-American.

emancipated from his former vulnerable self by promotion to this new, prestigious slavery.

H. S. Versnel's magisterial study of Isis the liberator and enslaver has revealed the wide currency of this paradox in both the religious and the political spheres during the Hellenistic period.[55] By the time of Apulcius the paradox has been intensified into a *coincidentia oppositorum,* and one of the texts that point in this direction is the New Testament.[56]

The traditional view that early Christianity spread most quickly among the slave population, a view that no doubt influenced both Nietzsche and Hegel in their characterizations of Christianity as a slave religion, is no longer held.[57] Nor is it widely accepted that Christianity played a key role in the undermining of slavery as an institution.[58] Rather like the Stoics, the writers of the New Testament tended to regard legal slavery as insignificant compared to a metaphorical slavery to sin (which one should avoid) or to God (which one should accept): "If when you were called, you were a slave, do not think it matters – even if you have a chance of freedom, you should prefer to make full use of your condition as a slave" (1 Corinthians 7.21ff.).[59]

But one cannot help being struck by the importance of figures from slavery in the New Testament (sometimes occluded by the tendency of translators to render *doulos* as "servant").[60] The parables of the conscientious steward (=*vilicus*; Mat. 24.45ff., Luke 12.41–48), of the crafty steward (Luke 16.1ff.), and of the talents (Luke 19.15) are all about slaves.[61] Matthew's "servant of two masters" (6.24, cf. Luke 16.13) may remind us of the slave in the Plautine household, with the difference that this metaphorical slave is subject to the incompatibles God and money, rather than father and son or husband and wife. Most interesting, for our purposes, is the paradoxical nature of the figure of slavery in the New Testament. Christ himself, the god who had humbled himself to become man, was a paradoxical figure "Who, though he was in the form of God,

---

[55] Versnel (1990), 39–95.   [56] Versnel (1990), 88–94.

[57] See Lane Fox (1986), 293–312 on the social makeup of the early Church.

[58] Texts and discussion in Garnsey (1996), 157–235. Shorter discussion in Lane Fox (1986), 295–9.

[59] Compare Paul's letter to Philemon, returning the escaped slave Onesimus, and Eph.6.5 "Slaves, be obedient to those who are, by human reckoning, your masters" (cf. Col. 3.22, Tit. 2.9.1, Pe. 2.18, 1 Tim. 6.1).   [60] Beavis (1992), 40.

[61] Complete list in Beavis (1992), 37.

did not count equality with God a thing to be grasped. But emptied himself, taking the form of a slave, being born in the likeness of men" (Philippians 2.6–7).[62] Paul, who is particularly obsessed with the figure of slavery, uses it, like the priest of Isis, as a figure both of what Christ has delivered us from (e.g. Romans 6.6, 8.21) and of our proper relation to Christ. In "Peter," these two valences are condensed into a paradox like the priest of Isis' *in servitutem vindicavit*: "behave like free men, not using your freedom as an excuse for wickedness, but as slaves of God" (1 Peter 2.16). Paul writes to the Corinthians (1 Corinthians 22–3) "Anyone who when called was a free man is a slave of Christ. You have been bought at a price. Do not become slaves of any human." Since Christ has bought us as his slaves, we should not become the slaves of any mere human.[63] Martin (1990) argues that Paul's pride in calling himself the slave of Christ[64] not only derives from Old Testament usages but also reflects social realities in the Roman world, where to be the slave of a great man and, a fortiori, a god, could be a source of pride and power, preferable to being an insignificant freedman, or even, in many cases, free. These usages claim that the bearer is an agent of Christ or God and wields his authority. It is true that there were Jewish precedents for this figure, but consider the Roman themes in the metaphor of slavery that runs through Paul's letter to the Galatians: the Law was serving as a *paedagogus* to look after us, to lead us to Christ (3.24); an heir, during the time he is under age, is no different from a slave – so too were we, when we were children, enslaved to the elemental principles of the world (4.1–3);[65] Paul carries branded on his body the marks (*stigmata*) of Jesus (6.17).

Stigmata (literally "tattoos") refers to the humiliating and servile corporal punishment Paul has undergone as slave of Christ (2 Corinthians 11.23–4). Like a Plautine slave, he flaunts the marks of punishment proudly, but the comparison with Apuleius' hero is even closer. The very last sentence of the *Golden Ass* has Lucius going about his duties in Rome with the shaven head of the Isiac, "neither covering up nor hiding [his]

---

[62] Jesus in this respect is modeled on Isaiah's servant (52.13–53.12), in turn a figure for the people privileged to be slaves of God after being delivered from slavery in Egypt.

[63] Martin (1990), 63 points out that *agorazein* does not mean "redeemed," as it is often translated.

[64] Rom. 1:1; Phil. 1:1; Gal. 1:10; Acts 16:17.

[65] Garnsey (1997), 105–6 argues that this passage refers to the *tutela impuberis* (guardianship of a minor) in Roman law.

baldness, but displaying it wherever [he] went." The shaven head was associated not only with the Isiac priest (slave of the goddess) but also with the buffoon and the slave who has regained his freedom.[66]

The figure who looks out at us from the end of *Golden Ass*, proud of his divine humiliation, seems to straddle two worlds. But perhaps we exaggerate the extent of the gap between pagan and Christian. Bowersock (1994) has made a powerful argument that there are points of overlap and interchange between Christian and pagan literature. One of the themes he pursues is that of resurrection, almost a *topos* in the Greek novel. He cites a striking scene from Apuleius in which a boy rises from his tomb into the arms of his father by a process Apuleius calls *postliminium mortis*, alluding to the term in Roman law that covers the restitution of rights to a Roman who has been captured in war (and thus become, by Roman law, a slave) but has subsequently returned.[67] Apuleius is particularly fond of this word and uses it in another passage in the same sense (2.28); it also occurs several times as an adverb ("so as to restore the status quo"), once in the mouth of Fotis, when she tells Lucius how to reverse the spell that has turned him into an ass and become his old self again (*in meum Lucium postliminio redibis*, 3.24). In this respect, the story of Lucius resonates with the story of the god who humbled himself to take on a new form, became a slave and a human (Philippians 2.6–7), suffered, died and rose from the dead.

<hr>

[66] Winkler (1985), 225–6.
[67] Apuleius 10.12; Bowersock (1994), 108–10.

Epilogue

When Shakespeare's Speed tells his master Valentine that "though the Chameleon love can feed on air, I am one that am nourished by my victuals, and would fain have meat" (*Two Gentlemen of Verona* 2.1.180f.) he echoes many a Plautine slave mocking the absurdity of his master's amours.[1] European comedy knows the *servus callidus* in the *zanni* (clowns) of *Commedia dell'Arte*, the *fourbes* (knaves) of Molière, Beaumarchais' Figaro and a host of other literary servants, culminating in the Mr. Belvederes and Bensons of the American SitCom of the Eighties.[2] Though ancient drama did not feature the cheeky *soubrette* quite as prominently as did, for instance, Beaumarchais, the ancestry of Suzanne in *Le Mariage de Figaro* includes figures like *Casina*'s Pardalisca and Apuleius' Fotis.

Besides betraying their literary pedigree these figures also bear the marks, and pursue the agenda, of their own times. The eighteenth century is the golden age of the literary servant, but where the symbiotic duo of so much of Roman slave literature is trapped in endlessly repeatable routines that lead to no resolution, the servants of eighteenth-century literature are often going places. At the beginning of the century, Lesage's cynical and ruthless servant Frontin closes the play *Turcaret* (1709) with the words "Voilà le règne de M.Turcaret fini; le mien va commencer" and, at the end of the century (1784), Beaumarchais' Figaro presages the Revolution with an attack on the privileges of birth (Act 5, sc.1). Where Plautus's slaves compared themselves to playwrights, Figaro

---

[1] A parallel pointed out by McCarthy (forthcoming).

[2] Emelina (1975) and Klenke (1992).

actually has ambitions to be one. Robbins (1986) comments that "By the eighteenth century, the bourgeoisie had composed the subversive bits and pieces of hundreds of traditional servitors into such heroic portraits of its own servitude as Defoe's Moll and Richardson's Pamela, Lesage's Gil Blas and Beaumarchais' Figaro" (80).

The novels of Defoe, Richardson and Lesage are the descendants of, among others, the Greek romantic novel and Apuleius' *Golden Ass*. Lesage's *Gil Blas* is usually assigned to the genre of the picaresque, and it is with the prototype of the picaresque, *Lazarillo de Tormes* (1554), that the modern novel begins to tell the *story* of the servant and to conceive of the servant as having a life. In this enterprise, the *Life of Aesop* is also an important ancient influence, and at least one of the incidents in *Lazarillo* can be traced back to an origin in the *Life*.[3] Richardson's Pamela, a servant abducted by her enamored, arrogant and tyrannical master, has a lineage that can be traced to the abducted and enslaved heroines of the Greek romantic novel, with the differences that Pamela *begins* as a servant (but ends as her master's wife) and, instead of being abducted *from* her lover, she is abducted *by* him. It is not so much the restoration of the status quo that is at issue here as the ascension of Pamela to her rightful place, which is above her station. But Richardson echoes the Greek novelists in making Pamela's sexual virtue the main proof that she is no servant.[4]

Finally, servants and masters in modern literature play metapoetic roles just like their Roman counterparts. One of the most interesting examples, which actually cites an ancient text, occurs in Diderot's *Jacques le Fataliste*. In Diderot's novel, Jacques and his master pursue their travels while the master importunes his servant to tell the story of his loves, which unfolds piecemeal, constantly interrupted by chance events and other tales; shadowing this relation is an intermittent dialogue between narrator and imaginary audience, the audience making all manner of literal-minded demands on the author and evincing the same bald curiosity as Jacques' master. The narrator resists these demands just as Jacques accedes only reluctantly to his master's promptings; he is not a slave, or if he is, he is a very Aesop. In one of these imaginary inter-

---

[3] Holzberg (1992), ix–x.
[4] Doody (1996) makes an impressive argument that Classical prose fiction plays an important role in the history of the novel.

changes the narrator answers the reader's "Where in god's name were they going?" by asking "Does anybody ever know where they are going? What about you?" and then launches into a story from the *Life of Aesop*. Sent by his master to see if the baths were crowded, Aesop was accosted by the town guard who asked him where he was going. Aesop replied that he didn't know and the guard hauled him off to prison. "There you are," said Aesop, "Didn't I tell you I didn't know where I was going? I wanted to go to the baths, and here I am going to prison." Diderot concludes "Jacques followed his master like you follow yours."[5] Aesop has really controlled this interchange, in which the power of authority has been folded back into Aesop's knowledge. He has turned the account he is required to give of himself into a prediction that brings about its own fufillment. So Diderot's narrator provokes the imperious reader to demand that the narrator give an account of himself (where is he going?) only to remind that reader that he will follow the story wherever it goes, just as Jacques follows his master, or the town guard of Athens follows Aesop's script.

The writer's identification with the servant looks rather different if we shift the scene from eighteenth-century France to nineteenth-century America, where the servant may be a slave. Stephen Railton makes some penetrating criticisms of white writers' appropriation of slavery as a metaphor for their frustrations at the hands of an uncomprehending audience, an appropriation that was hardly fitting at a time when the fate of the slave was such an immediate and real issue.[6] Melville's "Benito Cereno" is Railton's prime example of this appropriation, a difficult, modernist short story about a slave revolt, rife with epistemological ironies. Discussing the canonical status of this story, Railton contrasts the aesthetic demands it places on the reader with the very different imaginative demands on the white reader made by the ex-slave Frederick Douglass in his more communicative story about a slave revolt; those demands are signalled by Douglass's title, "The Heroic Slave." Railton asks why the prestige of one kind of difficulty has flourished at the expense of the other. As I said at the beginning of this book, students of Latin literature are not faced with a choice between reading the master's or the slave's account of slavery. The task that I have set myself here is to

---

[5] Diderot (1986), 58–9.   [6] Railton (1991), 190–201.

let a certain agenda of Roman literature come into focus, namely the agenda of the slaveowner. But the danger of the material I have assembled is that it may make of slavery a subject understood exclusively from the perspective of the masters. In this context the slave narratives of nineteenth-century America provide a needed corrective to the bias of Roman literature. At the beginning of this study (p. 5) I cited, as evidence of the affective unit formed by the ancient Roman household, the fact that Cato had his wife suckle slave children together with his own "to encourage brotherly feelings in them towards her own son." It takes Harriet Jacobs's harrowing narrative of her experience as a slave in a Southern household to bring home to us the dark side of this affective unit. Her *Incidents in the Life of a Slave Girl* describes vividly what it means for a slave, brought up as the foster-sibling of the free child, to discover suddenly that they have such cruelly divergent destinies, that she is the slave of her own playfellow.[7] The slave narrative not only reminds us of the perspective missing from the Roman literary record, it also alerts us to the ways in which that lack may distort our understanding of ancient slavery.

[7] Gates (1987) 363.

Bibliography

Anderson, W. S. (1993) *Barbarian Play: Plautus' Roman Comedy*. Berkeley
  (1995) "The Roman Transformation of Greek Domestic Comedy," *Classical World* 88,3: 171–80
Andreau, J. (1993) "The Freedman" in A. Giardina (ed.), 175–98
Bakhtin, M. (1968) *Rabelais and his World*, tr. H. Iswolsky. Cambridge, Mass.
  (1981) *The Dialogic Imagination*, tr. M. Holquist. Austin
Barrow, R. H. (1928) *Slavery in the Roman Empire*. London
Bartsch, S. (1989) *Decoding the Ancient Novel*. Princeton
Beavis, M. (1992) "Ancient Slavery as an Interpretive Context for the New Testament Servant Parables with Special Reference to the Unjust Steward (Luke 16:1–8)," *Journal of Biblical Literature* 111,1: 37–54
Benveniste, E. (1936) "*Liber* et *Liberi*," *Revue des Etudes Latines* 14: 53–8
Bernstein, M. (1992) *Bitter Carnival: Ressentiment and the Abject Hero*. Princeton
Bloomer, M. (1997) *Latinity and Literary Society at Rome*. Philadelphia
Bodel, J. (1994) "Trimalchio's Underworld" in J. Tatum (ed.), *The Search for the Ancient Novel*. Baltimore, 237–59
Bömer, F. (1981) *Untersuchungen über die Religion der Sklaven in Griechenland und Rom. Erster Teil: Die wichtigsten Kulte und Religionen in Rom und im Lateinischen Westen*. 2nd edn, Wiesbaden
Booth, A. (1979) "The Schooling of Slaves in First-Century Rome," *Transactions of the American Philological Association* 109:11–19
Boswell, J. (1988) *The Kindness of Strangers: The Abandonment of Children in Western Europe from Late Antiquity to the Renaissance*. New York
Bowersock, G. W. (1994) *Fiction as History: Nero to Julian*. Berkeley
Bradley, K. R. (1986) "Seneca and Slavery," *Classica et Mediaevalia* 37: 161–72
  (1987) *Slaves and Masters in the Roman Empire: a Study in Social Control*. Oxford
  (1990) "Servus Onerosus: Roman Law and the Troublesome Slave," *Slavery and Abolition* 11: 135–57
  (1991) *Discovering the Roman Family*. Oxford
  (1994) *Slavery and Society at Rome*. Cambridge

Brophy, R. (1975) "*Emancipatus Feminae*: a Legal Metaphor in Horace and Plautus," *Transactions of the American Philological Association* 105: 1-11

Brown, P. (1967) *Augustine of Hippo*. Berkeley

Brunt, P. A. (1971) *Italian Manpower 225 BC–AD 14*. Oxford
  (1980) "Evidence given under torture in the Principate," *Zeitschrift der Savigny Stiftung für Rechtsgeschichte* (*Rom. Abt.*) 97:256–65

Buckland, W. W. (1908) *The Roman Law of Slavery*. Cambridge

Cambiano, G. (1987) "Aristotle and Slavery" in M. I. Finley (ed.), *Classical Slavery*. London, 21– 41

Christes, J. (1979) "Reflexe erlebter Unfreiheit in den Sentenzen des Publilius Syrus," *Hermes* 107,2: 199–220

Clausen, W. (1994) *A Commentary on Virgil, Eclogues*. Oxford

Copley, F. O. (1947) "*Servitium Amoris* in the Roman Elegists," *Transactions of the American Philological Association* 78: 285–300

Courtney, E. (1995) *Musa Lapidaria: a Selection of Latin Verse Inscriptions*. Atlanta

D'Arms, J. H. (1991) "Slaves at Roman *convivia*," in W. J. Slater (ed.), *Dining in a Classical Context*. Ann Arbor, 171–83

Daviault, A. (1981) *Comoedia Togata: Fragments*. Paris

DeFilippo, J. (1990) "*Curiositas* and the Platonism of Apuleius' *Golden Ass*," *American Journal of Philology* 111: 471–92

Diderot, D. (1986) *Jacques the Fatalist* (tr. M. Henry). London

Dionisotti, A. C. (1982) "From Ausonius' Schooldays? A Schoolbook and its Relatives," *Journal of Roman Studies* 72: 83–125

Doody, M. (1996) *The True Story of the Novel*. New Brunswick

DuBois, P. (1991) *Torture and Truth*. London

Du Bois, W. E. B. (1997) *The Souls of Black Folk*, eds. D. Blight and R. Gooding-Williams. Boston

Duff, J. W and Duff, A. M. (1935) *Minor Latin Poets*, vol. 1. Cambridge, Mass.

Dumont, J. (1987) *Servus: Rome et l'Esclavage sous la Republique*. Rome

Dupont, F. (1992) *Daily Life in Ancient Rome*. Oxford

Eagleton, T. (1991) *Ideology: an Introduction*. London

Eck, W. and Heinrichs, J. (1993) *Sklaven und Freigelassene in der Gesellschaft der römischen Kaiserzeit*. Darmstadt

Edwards, C. (1993) *The Politics of Immorality in Ancient Rome*. Cambridge
  (1997) "Unspeakable Professions: Public Performance and Prostitution in Ancient Rome," in J. Hallett and M. Skinner (eds.), *Roman Sexualities*. Princeton, 66-95

Emelina, J. (1975) *Les Valets et les servantes dans le théâtre comique en France de 1610 à 1700*. Grenoble

Fabre, G. (1981) *Libertus: recherches sur les rapports patron-affranchi à la fin de la Republique romaine*. Paris

Fairchild, C. (1984) *Domestic Enemies: Servants and their Masters in Old Regime France*. Baltimore

Finley, M. I. (1960) *Slavery in Classical Antiquity*. Cambridge
  (1973) *The Ancient Economy*. London

(1980) *Ancient Slavery and Modern Ideology*. New York

(1981) *Economy and Society in Ancient Greece*. London

Fitzgerald, W. (1989) "Horace, Pleasure and the Text," *Arethusa* 22.1: 81–104

(1995) *Catullan Provocations: Lyric Poetry and the Drama of Position*. Berkeley

(1996) "Labor and Laborer in Latin Poetry: the Case of the *Moretum*," *Arethusa* 29.3: 389–418.

Flusche, M. (1975) "Joel Chandler Harris and the Folklore of Slavery," *Journal of American Studies* 9: 347-63

Fraenkel, E. (1960) *Elementi Plautini in Plauto*. Florence

Gardner, J. (1993) *Being a Roman Citizen*. London

Garlan, Y. (1988) *Slavery in Ancient Greece* (tr. J. Hoyd). Ithaca

Garnsey, P. (1996) *Ideas of Slavery from Aristotle to Augustine*. Cambridge

(1997) "Slaves, Sons – and Christians," in B. Rawson and P. Weaver (eds.), *The Roman Family in Italy: Status, Sentiment, Space*. Oxford, 101–21.

Garrido-Hory, M. (1981) *Martial et l'esclavage*. Paris

Gates, H. L. (1987) *The Classic Slave Narratives*. New York

Genovese, E. D. (1972) *Roll, Jordan, Roll: The World the Slaves Made*. New York

George, M. (1997) "*Servus* and *domus*: the Slave in the Roman House," in R. Laurence and A. Wallace-Hadrill (eds.), *Domestic Space in the Roman World: Pompeii and Beyond*, Portsmouth, R.I., 15–24

Gianotti, G. F. (1986) *'Romanza' e Ideologia: Studi sulle Metamorfosi di Apuleio*. Naples

Giardina, A. (1993) *The Romans* (tr. L. Cochrane). Chicago

Gordon, M. L. (1968) "The Nationality of Slaves under the Early Roman Empire," in M. I. Finley (ed.), *Slavery in Classical Antiquity*. Cambridge and New York, 171–89

Green, R. H. P. (1991) *The Works of Ausonius*. Oxford

Guardi, T. 1974. "I precedenti greci alla figura del *servus currens* della comedia romana," *Pan* 2: 5–15

Habinek, T. (1990) "Towards a History of Friendly Advice: the Politics of Candor in Cicero's *De Amicitia*." *Apeiron* 23: 165–85.

Hanson, J. A. (1996) *Apuleius: Metamorphoses* (2 vols.). Cambridge, Mass.

Hegel, G. W. F. (1977) *Phenomenology of Spirit*, tr. A. V. Miller. Oxford

Henderson, J. (1991–92) "Wrapping up the Case: Reading Ovid *Amores* 2.7 (+8)," Part 1: *Materiali e Discussioni* 27: 38–88; Part 2: *Materiali e Discussioni* 28: 27–83

Hijmans, B. L. (1995) *"Curiositas"* in B. Hijmans et al. (eds.), *Apuleius Madaurensis, Metamorphoses: Book IX. Text, Introduction and Commentary*. Groningen, 362–79

Hinds, S. (1985) "Booking the Return Trip: Ovid and *Tristia* 1," *Proceedings of the Cambridge Philological Society* 31: 13–32

(1998) *Allusion and Intertext: Dynamics of Appropriation in Roman Poetry*. Cambridge

Hock, R. (1988) "Servile Behavior in Sallust's *Bellum Catilinae*," *Classical World* 82.1: 13–24

Holzberg, N., ed. (1992) *Der Aesop-Roman: Motivgeschichte und Erzählstruktur*. Tübingen

(1993) *Die Antike Fabel: ein Einführung*. Darmstadt
Hopkins, K. (1978) *Conquerors and Slaves*. Cambridge
  (1993) "Novel Evidence for Roman Slavery," *Past and Present* 138: 3–27
Hunter, V. (1992) "Constructing the Body of the Citizen: Corporal Punishment in Classical Athens," *Echos du Monde Classique/Classical Views* 36: 271–91
James, S. (1997) "Slave-Rape and Female Silence in Ovid's Love Poetry," *Helios* 24: 60–76
Jakobson, R. and Halle, M. (1971) (rev. edn.) *Fundamentals of Language*. The Hague
Johnson, W. R. (1993) *Horace and the Dialectic of Freedom: Readings in* Epistles 1. Ithaca
Jones, C. P. (1987) "Stigma: Tattooing and Branding in Greco-Roman Antiquity," *Journal of Roman Studies* 77: 139–55.
Jory, E. J. (1966) "*Dominus Gregis?*" *Classical Philology* 61: 102–4
Joshel, S. (1986) "Nurturing the Master's Child: Slavery and the Roman Child-Nurse," *Signs* 12,1: 3–22.
  (1992) *Work, Identity and Legal Status at Rome*. Norman
Just, R. (1985) "Freedom, Slavery and the Female Psyche," in *Crux: Essays in Greek History Presented to G.E.M. de Sainte Croix*, P. A. Cartledge and F. D. Harvey (eds.). Exeter, 169–88
Kenney, E. J. (1990) "Psyche and her Mysterious Husband," in D. A. Russell (ed.), *Antonine Literature*. Oxford, 175–98
Klenke, D. (1992) *Herr und Diener in der französischen Komödie des 17. und 18. Jahrhunderts: Eine ideologische Studie*. Frankfurt
Kolendo, J. (1981) "L'esclavage et la vie sexuelle des hommes libres à Rome," *Quaderni Camerti di Studi Romanistici* 10: 288–97
Kudlien, F. (1986) "Empticius Servus: Bemerkungen zur antiken Sklavenmarkt," *Historia* 35: 240– 56
  (1991) *Sklavenmentalität im Spiegel Antiker Wahrsagerei*. Stuttgart
Labate, M. (1984) *L'arte di farsi amare: Modelli culturali e progetto didascalico nell' elegia ovidiana*. Pisa
Lacey, W. K. (1986) "*Patria Potestas*," in B. Rawson (ed.), *The Family in Ancient Rome: New Perspectives*. Ithaca, 121–44
Lane Fox, R. L. (1986) *Pagans and Christians*. Harmondsworth
Levin, H. (1966) *The Gates of Horn: a Study of Five French Realists*. New York
Lott, E. (1995) *Love and Theft: Blackface Minstrelsy and the American Working Class*. Oxford
Lowrie, M. (1997) *Horace's Narrative Odes*. Oxford
Lyne, R. O. A. M. (1979) "Servitium Amoris," *Classical Quarterly* n.s. 29: 117–30.
McCarthy, K. (1998) "*Servitium amoris: Amor servitii*", in Murnaghan and Joshel (1998), 174-92
  (forthcoming) *Slaves, Masters and the Art of Authority in Plautine Comedy*. Princeton
Manning, C. (1989) "Stoicism and Slavery in the Roman Empire," *ANRW* II.36.3: 1518–63
Martin, D. A. (1990) *Slavery as Salvation: the Metaphor of Slavery in Pauline Christianity*. New Haven

Mélèze-Modrzejewski, J. (1975) "Hommes libres et bêtes dans les droits antiques," in
    L. Poliakov (ed.), *Hommes et bêtes: entretiens sur le racisme*, Paris, 75–102
Muecke, F. (1993) *Horace: Satires II*. Warminster
Murgatroyd, P. (1981) "*Servitium Amoris* and the Roman Elegists," *Latomus* 49:
    589–606
Murnaghan, S. and Joshel, S. (1998) *Women and Slaves in Greco-Roman Culture*.
    London
Norden, Fritz von (1912) *Apulejus von Madaura und das römische Privatrecht*. Leipzig
Oliensis, E. (1995) "Life After Publication: Horace *Epistles* 1.20," *Arethusa* 28:
    209–24.
    (1998) *Horace and the Rhetoric of Authority*. London
Parker, H. (1989) "Crucially Funny, or Tranio on the Couch: the *Servus Callidus* and
    Jokes About Torture," *Transactions of the American Philological Association* 119:
    233–46.
    (1998) "Loyal Slaves and Loyal Wives" in Joshel and Murnaghan (1998), 152–73.
Patterson, O. (1982) *Slavery and Social Death: a Comparative Study*. Cambridge, Mass
    (1991) *Freedom: Volume 1: Freedom in the Making*. New York
Penwill, J. (1975) "Slavish Pleasure and Profitless Curiosity: Fall and Redemption in
    Apuleius' Metamorphoses,' *Ramus* 4:49-82
Perry, B. (1952) *Aesopica: a series of texts relating to Aesop or ascribed to him or closely
    connected with the literary tradition that bears his name*. Urbana
Raaflaub, K. (1985) *Die Entdeckung der Freiheit: Zur historischen Semantik und
    Gesellschaftsgeschichte eines politischen Grundbegriffes der Griechen*. Munich
Rabinowitz, N. (1998) "Slaves with slaves: Women and class in Euripidean Tragedy,"
    in Murnaghan and Joshel (1998), 56–68.
Railton, Stephen. (1991) *Authorship and Audience: Literary Performance in the
    American Renaissance*. Princeton
Rawson, B. (ed.) (1986) *The Family in Ancient Rome: New Perspectives*. Ithaca
Rawson, E. (1993) "Freedmen in Roman Comedy," in R. Scodel (ed.), *Theater and
    Society in the Classical World*. Ann Arbor, 215–33
Rei, A. (1998) "Villains, wives and slaves in the comedy of Plautus," in Murnaghan and
    Joshel, 92-108
Robbins, B. (1993) *The Servant's Hand: English Fiction from Below*. New York
Saller, R. (1982) *Personal Patronage Under the Early Roman Empire*. Cambridge
    (1987) "Slavery and the Roman Family" in M. I. Finley (ed.), *Classical Slavery*.
    London, 65–87
    (1994) *Patriarchy, Property and Death in the Roman Family*. Cambridge
    (1996) "The hierarchical household in Roman society: a study of domestic slavery,"
    in M. L. Bush (ed.) *Serfdom and Slavery: Studies in Legal Bondage*. London,
    112–29
Sandy, G. (1974) "*Serviles voluptates* in Apuleius' *Metamorphoses*," *Phoenix* 28:
    234–44
Scheidel, W. (1997) "Quantifying the sources of slaves in the Early Roman Empire,"
    Journal of Roman Studies 87:156-69
Schlam, C. (1992) *The Metamorphoses of Apuleius: On Making an Ass of Oneself*. Chapel Hill

Segal, E. (1987) *Roman Laughter: the Comedy of Plautus*. 2nd edn. Cambridge, Mass

Sharrock, A. (1993) "The Art of Deceit: Pseudolus and the Nature of Reading," *Classical Quarterly* 46 : 153–74.

Shipp, G. P. (1953) "Greek in Plautus," *Wiener Studien* 66: 105–12

Shumate, N. (1996) *Crisis and Conversion in Apuleius' Metamorphoses*. Ann Arbor

Slater, N. (1985) *Plautus in Performance: The Theater of the Mind*. Princeton

Slater, W. (1974) "*Pueri, Turba Minuta*," *Bulletin of the Institute of Classical Studies of the University of London* 21: 133–40

Spranger, P. (1961) *Historische Untersuchungen zu den Sklavenfiguren des Plautus und Terenz*. Mainz

Stallybrass, P. and White, A. (1986) *The Politics and Poetics of Transgression*. Cornell

Starr, R. (1991) "Reading Aloud: *Lectores* and Roman Reading," *Classical Journal* 86: 337–43.

de Ste Croix, G. E. M. (1981) *The Class Struggle in the Ancient Greek World*. Ithaca and London

Stephens, S. and Winkler, J. (1995) *Ancient Greek Novels: the Fragments*. Princeton

Stone, L. (1977) *The Family, Sex and Marriage in England, 1500-1800*. London

Teitler, H. C. (1985) *Notarii and Exceptores*. Amsterdam

Thalmann, W. (1997) "Versions of Slavery in the *Captivi* of Plautus," *Ramus* 25,2: 112–45

Thebert, Y. (1993) "The Slave," in A. Giardina (ed.), 138–74.

Treggiari, S. (1969) *Roman Freedmen during the Late Republic*. Oxford

 (1979) "Questions on Women Domestics in the West," in *Schiavitù, manomissione e classi dipendenti nel mondo antico*. Rome, 185–201

 (1981) "Concubinae," *Papers of the British School at Rome* 49:59-81

 (1991) *Roman marriage: Iusti Coniuges from the Time of Cicero to the Time of Ulpian*. Oxford

Versnel, H. (1990) *Inconsistencies in Greek and Roman Religion, 1: Ter Unus: Isis, Dionysos, Hermes. Three Studies in Henotheism*. Leiden

 (1993) *Inconsistencies in Greek and Roman Religion, 2: Transition and Reversal in Myth and Ritual*. Leiden

Veyne, P. (1961) "Vie de Trimalcion," *Annales* 16: 213–37

 (1987) "The Roman Empire," in P. Aries and G. Duby (eds.), *A History of Private Life*, Vol. 1: *From Pagan Rome to Byzantium*. Cambridge, Mass., 1–233.

 (1988) *Roman Erotic Elegy: Love, Poetry and the West*, tr. D. Pellauer. Chicago

Vlastos, G. (1941) "Slavery in Plato's Republic," *The Philosophical Review* 50: 289–304 (reprinted in Finley 1960).

Vogt, J. and Bellen, H. (eds.) (1983) *Bibliographie zur Antiken Sklaverei*. Bochum

Wallace-Hadrill, A. (1994) *Houses and Society in Pompeii and Herculaneum*. Princeton

Walsh, P. G. (1981) "Apuleius and Plutarch," in H. Blumenthal and R. Markus (eds.), *Neoplatonism and Early Christian Thought*. London, 20–32

Walters, J. (1997). "Invading the Roman Body: Manliness and Impenetrability in Roman Thought," in J. Hallett and M. Skinner (eds.), *Roman Sexualities*. Princeton, 29–43.

Watson, A. (1987) *Roman Slave Law*. Baltimore

West, D. (1995) *Horace, Odes 1: Carpe Diem*. Oxford

White, P. (1993) *Promised Verse: Poets in the Society of Augustan Rome*. Cambridge, Mass.

Wiedemann, T. (1981) *Greek and Roman Slavery*. Baltimore

(1985) "The Regularity of Manumission at Rome," *Classical Quarterly* 35: 162–75.

(1987) *Slavery: Greece and Rome*. Oxford

Wiles, D. (1988) "Greek Theater and the Legitimation of Slavery," in L. Archer (ed.), *Slavery and Other Forms of Unfree Labor*. London and New York, 53–67

Williams, G. (1995) "*Libertino Patre Natus*: True or False?" in S. J. Harrison (ed.), *Homage to Horace: a Bimillenary Celebration*. Oxford, 296–313

Williams, R. (1983) *Keywords: A Vocabulary of Culture and Society* (rev. edn.) Oxford

Winkler, J. (1985) *Auctor and Actor: a Narratological Reading of Apuleius's* The Golden Ass. Berkeley

Wirszubski, C. (1960) *Libertas as a Political Idea at Rome During the Late Republic and Early Principate*. Cambridge

Yardley, J. C. (1974) "Propertius' Lycinna," *Transactions of the American Philological Association* 104: 429–34

General index

Index of passages discussed